AMAZON PUBLISHING MANUAL

EXPLORING AMAZON'S TOOLS TO HELP YOU PUBLISH AND PROMOTE YOUR BOOK

TIM FLANAGAN

Also by Tim Flanagan

The Moon Stealers and the Quest for the Silver Bough (Book 1)
The Moon Stealers and the Queen of the Underworld (Book 2)
The Moon Stealers and The Everlasting Night (Book 3)
The Moon Stealers and The Children of the Light (Book 4)

The Curious Disappearance of Professor Brown
The Mystery of Van Gogh's Missing Heart
Lawrence Pinkley's Casebook Vol. 1
Lawrence Pinkley's Casebook Vol. 2

Amazon Publishing Manual
Copyright © 2015 Tim Flanagan

Published 2015 by Flanagan Wale Publishing

ISBN-13: 978-1514631898
ISBN-10: 151463189X

AMAZON PUBLISHING MANUAL

EXPLORING AMAZON'S TOOLS TO HELP YOU PUBLISH AND PROMOTE YOUR BOOK

TIM FLANAGAN

About The Author

Tim Flanagan is a self published author with numerous titles under his name. He is also the Creative Director at Novel Design Studio, a company that specializes in supporting traditional and self published authors by providing cover design, eBook formatting, Amazon optimization, website creation, and advertising.

Recently he teamed up with market leading book promoter, Nick Wale to set up Flanagan Wale Publishing. They now have a growing team of authors who benefit from ground breaking author contracts, and regularly score top ranking positions across a variety of Amazon categories.

Flanagan Wale Publishing are always on the look out for new and exciting writers. Why not contact us and tell us about your book:

publishingteam@flanaganwalepublishing.com

CONTENTS

Introduction..13

PART ONE: PREPARING FOR PUBLICATION

1. Setting Up Your KDP Account 19
Step 1. Opening A KDP Account...19
Step 2. Completing Your Personal Information 20
Step 3. Complete Your Tax Information 21
Step 4. Complete Your Royalty Payments 22

2. KDP Select 27
How To Join KDP 28
Kindle Unlimited...29
Kindle Owners' Lending Library (KOLL) 30
KDP Select Global Fund..31
KDP Select All-Stars..32
Free Book Deal...33
Kindle Countdown Deals 34
    How To Schedule A Kindle Countdown Deal Or Free Book Promotion......................35

3. Preparing The Inside Of Your Book.................................39
Front Matter 39
Acceptable File Formats 39
    Microsoft Word 40
    Mobi Format 40

4. Kindle Kids' Book Creator 42
How To Build A Children's Picture Book...............................42
    Adding pages..45
    Deleting Pages 45
    Changing Book Settings 46
    Adding Text 46
    Adding additional Fonts 47
    Saving and Publishing 48

5. Kindle Textbook Creator..**49**
Download Kindle Textbook Creator...50
Creating A New Textbook..50
    Adding A Page..51
    Deleting a Page..51
    Reordering Pages...51
    Adding Images...51
    Adding Videos..52
    Adding Audio..52
    Creating A Table of Contents 53
    Previewing Your Book 54
    Saving And Exporting Your Textbook......................................55
Making Your Book Appear In The Textbook Category On Amazon 56

6. Kindle Comic Creator..**57**
Download Kindle Comic Creator..57
Create A New Book 58
    Screen Layout 59
    Adding Pages...59
    Deleting Pages...60
    Rearranging Your Pages 60
    Naming Your Pages 60
    Changing Book Settings 60
To Create A Panel 61
    To Create A Text Panel 62
    Adding Additional Fonts 63
Creating A Landscape Orientation Comic 63
Saving Your Project...65
    Building And Previewing Your Book 65

7. Kindle Previewer **66**
Download Kindle Previewer..66
Opening A Book...66
Viewing On Different Devices 69

8. Preparing Your Cover **70**

9. Cover Creator **71**
How To Create Your Cover 71
    Step 1. Choose Your Design 72
    Step 2. Style & Edit..72
    Step 3. Preview 73

10. Creating A Great Product Description **74**

Suggested Layout Of Your Book Description 74
Use html Formatting Tags To Change The Appearance Of The Wording 76
    Amazon Approved html Tags 76
    html Tag Example: 77

11. ISBN Numbers 79

12. Choosing Categories 80

13. Sub Category Keywords 82
Choosing your sub category keywords 82

14. Keywords 84
How To Use Amazon's Search Engine 84

15. Pre-Orders 89

16. Amazon Royalties 91
Getting Paid 91
Choosing A Royalty Percentage 91
How Are Royalties Calculated 93
VAT On List Prices 93

17. Kindle Matchbook 94

18. Kindle Book Lending 95

19. Publishing Your Book 96
1. Enter Your Book Details 97
2. Verify Your Publishing Rights 99
3. Target Your Book To Customers 100
4. Select Your Book Release Option 102
5. Upload Or Create A Book Cover 102
6. Upload Your Book File 103
7. Preview Your Book 104
8. Verify Your Publishing Territories 106
9. Set Your Pricing And Royalty 107
10. Kindle Matchbook 109
11. Kindle Book Lending 109

PART TWO: ONLINE TOOLS

20. Ranking 113

21. Reports 115
Sales Dashboard 115
Prior Six Weeks Royalties 116
Promotions 117
Ad Campaigns 117
Month-To-Date Unit Sales 118
Prior Months' Royalties 119
Payments 120
Pre Order Report 121

22. Look Inside 122

23. Author Central 123
How To Set Up Your Amazon.com Author Central Page 124
Build Your Amazon Author page 125
   Add A Biography 125
   Add A Blog Feed 125
   Add Events 126
   Add An Author Page URL 127
   Add Photos 128
   Add Videos 129
   Add A Twitter Feed 131
Add Your books 132
Sales Information 132
   Nielsen BookScan 133
   Sales Rank 133
   Author Rank 134
Customer Reviews 135

24. Kindle Singles 136
Submission Criteria 137
How To Submit 137

25. Kindle Worlds 139

26. Amazon Marketing 141
Target Your Ad 143
Set Your Campaign Name, Bid and Budget 145
Campaign Settings 146

Preview Your Ad...147
Payment Settings 147

27. Price Matching 149
Using Price Matching To Create A Permafree Book 149

28. Amazon Cart 151
How Readers Can Set Up Amazon Cart 151

29. Amazon Associates 153
Setting Up Your Account 153
Your Payment Method 153
Creating Links 155

30. Adjusting Your Book Details 157
Updating Your Book Description 157
Update The Contents Of The Book 157
Update Series Title 157
Updating Sub Title 158
Change The Price..158
Adjust The Categories 158
Adjusting Keywords 158
Expand Author Central 158

31. Kindle Scout...159
Submitting To Kindle Scout 160

APPENDICES

Appendix A Categories - Fiction 165

Appendix B Categories - Juvenile Fiction.....................167

Appendix C Categories - Non Fiction 171

Appendix D Sub Categories - Fiction 218

Appendix E Sub Categories - Non Fiction 232

Appendix F 49 Free Websites That Will Promote Your Free Book 243

Appendix G Download Addresses................................249

Introduction

Before we go any further, let's get one thing straight - this is not a book that pretends to tell you how to get rich quick by publishing a book, or letting you into a little known secret that can beat Amazon at their own game. There are plenty of other books for you to waste your money on that make those claims, but this is not one of them.

This is also not a book that tells you how to write a bestseller, it won't tell you how to develop your characters or improve the story structure.

So, what is this book about?

This is a book that explores all of the different programmes, options and systems that are available to you as an Amazon author. There is no mystery or conspiracy - Amazon want you to sell your books as much as you do because they make money on every sale. It's simple business sense. It's in their interests to make the process as easy as possible and give you the chance to promote your books alongside the big sellers. This guide takes you through the basics if you are a beginner, or introduces you to new areas of publishing on Amazon that you might not have explored yet. It is an Amazon resource book where everything is collected in one place.

But, I know what you are thinking - *Amazon changes so quickly that this book will soon be out of date*. Not necessarily. This paperback version will be updated at intervals, but the Kindle version will be updated a lot more frequently. If you download the Kindle version you can adjust the settings so that every update I make to the Kindle base file will automatically be updated in your device. That way you get an ever evolving resource book.

If you don't know how to set your Kindle up to receive automatic updates, just follow these simple steps:

1. Log in to your Amazon account
2. Find the "Your Account" option at the top of the page

Hello, Timothy
Your Account ▾

3. In the drop down menu go down to "Manage Your Content and Devices"

Your Account

Your Orders

Your Wish List

Your Recommendations

Your Subscribe & Save Items

Your Prime Membership

Manage Your Content and Devices

Your Music Library

Your Cloud Drive
Free unlimited photo storage
for Prime members

Your Prime Instant Video
Unlimited streaming of thousands
of movies and TV shows

Your Watchlist

Your Video Library

Your Rental List

Your Games and Software Library

Your Apps & Devices

Not Timothy? Sign Out

4. Select the tab labeled "Settings"
5. Scroll down to "Automatic Book Update" and select "On".

And, that's it - every time Amazon changes anything or introduces a new product I will update the mobi file and your copy should automatically update too. What you've just done is also a great example of how this book works - simple and straightforward instructions with images to walk you to an achievable goal.

One more thing before we move on. Add your email address to the Amazon Publishing Manual database and I will let you know what improvements or additions have been made to the book so you don't need to manually keep going back and checking. Sign up by going to:

http://eepurl.com/blJOjz

As well as walk-through guides, there are also some Appendices at the back of the book which include useful lists as well as addresses for downloadable pdf files to help you as you work through certain aspects of publishing. These will also be added to and updated over time and as the need arises.

Inside this book the whole process of publishing on KDP is explained, together with the expanding range of options Amazon provide to help you promote your books. And, that is the biggest part of publishing a book - the marketing. When you're fighting against a tide of three million other books, the odds are against you. The best way forward? Study the marketplace you're going into, know what it has on offer and use it to your advantage.

That is the core purpose of this book - to provide you with knowledge of the platform you will be using to publish your book to the world.

PART ONE: PREPARING FOR PUBLICATION

1. Setting Up Your KDP Account

If you're thinking about publishing your book online, look no further than Amazon. Each country specific marketplace has massive volumes of traffic browsing their ever growing catalogue of products. And they're looking for books to read on their eReaders, tablets, phones and computers.

In just a short period of time your book can made be available to readers around the world, but first you need to set up a publishing account. Amazon have created KDP - Kindle Direct Publishing, a platform that provides you with a whole host of tools and resources that are free to use and will help you release your book and sell it to readers.

Opening a KDP account does not cost you anything. The reason is, Amazon want you to sell your books - it's in their interest to do so. They earn their money on fees associated with every book they sell and if a buyer is already on their website, chances are they will also purchase something else whilst they are there.

Although you might not have finished writing your Bestseller yet, there's no time to lose - set up your KDP account today and begin completing all the relevant information so that it is ready for the time when you have finished writing. To open a KDP account and get paid royalties you will need to include your tax information, regardless of whether you are a US citizen or not, before you can start publishing your books on Amazon.

Step 1. Opening A KDP Account

Go to https://kdp.amazon.com/ and sign in with your Amazon account details (email and password), or sign up if you don't already have an Amazon account.

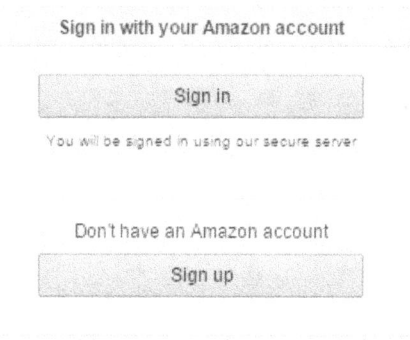

Now that you have opened your account you should see in the top right corner of your screen a box that says your account information is incomplete. Before you can publish anything you will need to complete all the relevant account details. Click "Update Now"

 Your account information is incomplete.
To publish a book, you will need to complete this. Update Now

---

Step 2. Completing Your Personal Information

The first thing you need to complete is your personal information, which is straightforward.

Your Account

> (i) To make your book available for sale (and so you can get paid for sales) on Amazon, please fill in the fields below. Once your account is complete, you can start publishing!

Company/Publisher Information

Full Name/Company Name (What's this?)	
Country	Select
Address Line 1	
Address Line 2 (optional)	
City	
State/Province/Region	
Zip/Postal Code	
Phone	

In the "Full Name / Company name" box write your own name here, or, if you've set up your own publishing company, insert that name instead. Complete your address and contact details.

If you scroll down the page your will see that the next section is concerning tax information.

Step 3. Complete Your Tax Information

Tax Information

 Incomplete

Amazon is required by US tax regulations to request information regarding your tax status under US law. Required US tax identification and information has not yet been submitted. Complete your tax information to begin publishing on Amazon.

Complete Tax Information

Tax Interview Help Guide

Once you have clicked on the "Complete Tax Information" button you will be taken through a series of pages that ask specific questions. Most of it is straightforward and self explanatory but it is essential for Amazon to create the tax forms that report your earnings. Without it they will not allow you to publish your books and sell them around the world.

The first question - "Are you, or are you not, a US Citizen", dictates what the following questions will be.

If you are a US Citizen:

Amazon will take the information you have already completed (name and address) and add it to the relevant form. Make sure it is accurate and matches exactly what details you complete for your US Income Tax Returns. You will need to select what Federal Tax Classification you fall into, as well as supplying your Tax Identification Number (TIN), including your Social Security Number (SSN - found on your Social Security Card) or Individual Tax Identification Number (ITIN - on the CP565 notice from IRS) or Employer Identification Number (EIN - on the CP575A notice from IRS).

This data is then used to complete your W-9 form. Review this information to make sure it is accurate then click "Save" to continue to the next page.

Amazon will then need to provide an electronic version of your tax information reporting form 1099-MISC to the IRS, but requires your consent. You will be able to obtain an electronic version of this form on or before January 31st each year. If you do not consent to an electronic version Amazon will mail a printed copy to the address you provided.

The next part is to consent to Form W-9. This can be done electronically, but if you prefer, you can print the form and send a signed copy to Amazon at: Amazon, Attn: Vendor Maintenance, PO Box 80683, Seattle, WA 98108-0683, USA.

Double check all information, particularly your name and TIN before submitting

If you are a non US citizen:

You need to define what type of beneficial owner you are. Most self published people will be classed as an individual. Complete your country of citizenship and your name as it appears on your tax return. Amazon will use the information you have already completed (name and address) for some parts of this form. You will need to declare whether you hold a valid US Green Card or have spent 31 days during the current year, or 183 days during the previous three year period in the US.

Declare if you have a US Tax Identification Number (TIN). Most self published authors who live outside of the US will need to check the box declaring you do not have a US TIN or foreign Income Tax Identification Number. This data is added into your W-8 Form. Review this information to make sure it is accurate then click "Save" to continue to the next page.

Amazon needs to provide an electronic version of your tax information reporting form 1042-S to the IRS, but require your consent. You will be able to obtain an electronic version of this form on or before March 15th each year. If you do not consent to an electronic version Amazon will mail a printed copy to the address you provided.

The next part is to consent to Form W-8. This can be done electronically, but if you prefer, you can print the form and send a signed copy to Amazon at: Amazon, Attn: Vendor Maintenance, PO Box 80683, Seattle, WA 98108-0683, USA.

Double check all information, before submitting the forms.

Step 4. Complete Your Royalty Payments

Move on to the Royalty Payment section.

Your Royalty Payments

Add a bank account in order to receive EFT or Wire payments (direct deposit) for royalty earned on Amazon marketplaces. Click here for more details. If you do not set-up a bank account, your royalties will be paid by check in the default currency of the marketplace. Be sure your royalty payment settings are correct before publishing a book, as your currency selection will be used to calculate your royalties as soon as a purchase occurs.

Your Bank Accounts

Add a bank account

Click on "Add a bank account". A separate window will open asking you to confirm which country your bank account is held in. This is important and will dictate what currency your royalties will be paid to you in. Each month your royalties will get converted from each different marketplace currency they were accrued in and exchanged into your local currency to be paid to you. For example if you live in the US, all your royalties, regardless of where they are generated will be converted to US dollars and credited to you.

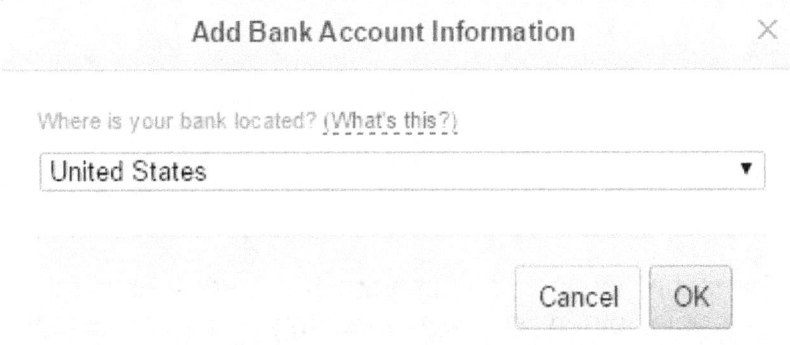

Once you have selected your country you will need to complete the rest of your bank account details.

Add Bank Account Information ✕

Where is your bank located? (What's this?)

| United Kingdom | ▼ |

Account holder name (exactly as it appears on account) (What's this?)

[   ]

Type of account ● Checking   ○ Savings

IBAN number (What's this?)

[   ]

BIC Code (What's this?)

[   ]

Name of bank

[   ]

Cancel   Done

The information you provide for your bank account needs to be as accurate as possible, otherwise payments may not be accepted by your bank. The easiest way to find out all the relevant information for this section is to look at one of your bank statements.

IBAN - Every bank account is given an International Bank Account Number, or IBAN. It consists of 15 to 31 letters and numbers. When you input that number here, do not include any spaces.

BIC - You also need to include the Bank Identifier Code or BIC. It consists of 8 to 11 letters and numbers. Sometimes this is also known as the SWIFT code.

When you have added the IBAN and BIC you need to input the name of the bank that holds your account. Click "Done" when you have finished and you will return to the royalties section where you can select how you want your royalties to be paid.

Under the "Amazon Marketplaces" section you will see all of the different locations where your book will be available. Beside the first option (amazon.com) you will see a small + symbol at the far right. Click this to open up the options for the amazon.com marketplace.

If you have completed your bank details it is likely that all of the Amazon marketplaces have been automatically completed so that you receive your royalty payments by Electronic Fund Transfer. However, you have a choice how you want your payments to be made.

There are three methods for most countries:

Check - to receive a check you will need to accrue a certain amount of royalties in your account before they are paid to you. For example, for amazon.com you will need $100 of sales before payment is released. Payments are made in the currency they were generated in. For example, if you receive £100 from amazon.co.uk you will receive your payment in British Pounds even if you live outside of Britain.

EFT - Electronic Fund Transfer. There is no restriction to the minimum volume of sales that you need to generate before you receive your payment when you elect to receive your money via EFT (except for royalties generated in Brazil). If you have completed your bank details, this option will have been automatically selected as your preferred payment option in your local currency. It is generally the easiest and quickest way to receive your royalties.

Wire - payment can be wired to your preferred bank account, but as with check payments you will need to accrue a certain level of royalties before payment is released. Your bank account may also charge you a fee for receiving wire payments. Payments can only be made in certain currencies and are only available in certain countries.

Royalty Payment Thresholds are summarized in the following table.

ROYALTY PAYMENT THRESHOLDS

Your local currency	Check Royalty Threshold	EFT Royalty Threshold		Wire Royalty Transfers
USD American Dollars	$100 USD	$0		Not available
GBP British Pounds	£100	£0		Not available
EUR Euro	€100	€0		Not available
CAD Canadian Dollars	$100 CAD	$0		$100 CAD
BRL Brazilian Real	$100 USD	R$20 for Brazilian Publishers	$100 / £100 / €100 for Non Brazilian Publishers	Not available
MXN Mexican Pesos	$100 USD	$0		$1,000 MXN
JPY Japanese Yen	$100 USD	¥0		Not available
INR Indian Rupee	$100 USD	Rs 0		Not available
AUR Australian Dollars	$100 USD	$0		$100 AUS
NZD New Zealand Dollars	$100 USD	Not available		$100 NSD

Click "Save" and your KDP account set up and ready to go.

2. KDP Select

This is an opt-in scheme that Amazon has designed to provide authors with the tools to reach a larger audience and take a greater share in royalties. But, it comes at a price. If you are enrolled on KDP Select, you have to provide exclusivity to Amazon. Your book cannot be available anywhere else on the internet in any other eBook form. This includes selling your book yourself from your own website. You can link your book from your website to your Amazon product page, but you cannot sell it directly from your website. This does not include paperback or hardback books. KDP Select is specific only to eBook versions of your book.

Some authors feel that exclusivity to Amazon restricts the potential reach of your book, but you have to weigh that up against the possible advantages that being in KDP Select will allow you.

What are the advantages to participating in KDP Select?

- **You can set your book for free for up to five days in every 90 days**. Potentially a free book will reach a wider audience. The only other way of doing this if you were not in KDP Select would be if Amazon price-matched your book as free on another sales channel. The lowest price you can sell your book is $0.99.

- **You will be able to earn a higher royalty in certain territories**. 70% royalty option is available for sales in Japan, India, Brazil and Mexico only if your book is enrolled on KDP Select. Sales in Australia, Canada, France, Germany, Italy, Netherlands, Spain, UK and US can earn 70% royalties whether you are enrolled on KDP Select or not.

- **Your book will automatically be available in the Kindle Owners' Lending Library**. When a reader borrows your book from the Lending Library you will receive a royalty from the KDP Select Global Fund.

- **Your book will be enrolled in Kindle Unlimited**. When a subscriber to Kindle Unlimited reads more than 10% of your book you will receive a royalty from the KDP Select Global Fund.

- **You will be able to use the Kindle Countdown Deal option**. This is a time restricted discounted price for your book that rises as the clock ticks towards the end of the deal.

- **You will have the option to participate in Amazon Marketing.** KDP Select books can be advertised across the amazon.com website on a pay-per-click basis.

How To Join KDP

When you're ready to upload your book to KDP, the first thing you will see when you "Add a New Title" is an option to enrol in the KDP Select programme. If you wish to commit your book to the scheme, just click the box beside "Enroll this book in KDP Select".

Introducing KDP Select

Take advantage of KDP Select, an optional program that makes your book exclusive to Kindle and eligible for the following benefits:

- **Reach more readers** - With each 90-day enrollment period, your book will appear in Kindle Unlimited in the U.S., U.K., Italy, Spain, Germany, France and Brazil and the Kindle Owners' Lending Library (KOLL) in the U.S, U.K., Germany, France, and Japan which can help readers discover your book.
- **Earn more money** - Every time your book is selected and read past 10% from Kindle Unlimited or borrowed from KOLL, you'll earn your share of the monthly KDP Select Global Fund. You can also earn a 70% royalty for sales to customers in Japan, Brazil, India and Mexico.
- **Maximize your sales potential** - Choose from two promotional tools including: Kindle Countdown Deals, time-bound promotional discounts for your book, available on Amazon.com and Amazon.co.uk, while earning royalties; or Free Book Promotion, where readers can get your book free for a limited time.

Learn more

☐ Enroll this book in KDP Select

By checking this box, you are enrolling in KDP Select for 90 days. Books enrolled in KDP Select must not be available in digital format on any other platform during their enrollment. If your book is found to be available elsewhere in digital format, it may not be eligible to remain in the program. See the KDP Select Terms and Conditions and KDP Select FAQs for more information.

If you enrol on KDP Select and Amazon discover your eBook is available elsewhere then they will send you a warning email asking you to remove it from the other site. If your book is still found to be available elsewhere they will automatically remove it from KDP Select, and possibly any other books you may have published through KDP even if they adhere to the exclusivity rule. Removal from KDP Select does not mean that your book will not be available on Amazon, it just means you will not have access to the promotional extras that KDP Select offers.

Any book can be enrolled in the KDP Select scheme, with the exception of books that you do not hold exclusive rights to which are deemed to be books that are already in the public domain. Any author in any country can enrol their book with KDP Select, but some of the promotional schemes are only available to Amazon customers in certain territories.

You do not have to enrol all of your books in KDP Select. You choose which books, if any, you wish to include.

Your book will be enrolled with KDP Select for 90 day periods during which Amazon must have exclusivity, even if you take your book out of KDP after more than 3 days. The 90 day period will automatically be renewed unless you uncheck the enrolment box in the Book Details Pages.

On the reports page of your KDP dashboard you will be able to see the number of people who borrowed your book from the Kindle Owners' Lending Library, as well as the number of people who read more than 10% of your book through the Kindle Unlimited Scheme. You will not be able to see the actual number of people who downloaded the book through Kindle Unlimited, only those who read a sufficient amount of the book.

Kindle Unlimited

Kindle Unlimited is a subscription service where readers pay a monthly fee which entitles them to download any book that is participating in the Kindle Unlimited scheme for free. As an author, you will receive a royalty payment from the KDP Select Global Fund whenever a reader reads more than 10% of the book. Kindle Unlimited subscribers can keep your book as long as they want. You will only get paid once after they have read more than 10%.

Subscribers to Kindle Unlimited can search for books that are enrolled on the scheme by visiting the specific Kindle Unlimited page, which you can find on the left of the Kindle Store page.

Popular Features

Kindle Unlimited

Kindle Best Sellers

Kindle Singles

Kindle Select 25

The Amazon Book Review

New York Times® Best Sellers

Editors' Picks

Short Reads

Kindle First

Kindle Worlds

Spanish eBooks

If you decided to use KDP Select your book will automatically be enrolled in the Kindle Unlimited scheme which is currently only available to Amazon customers in the US, UK, Germany, Spain, France, Italy, Canada, Mexico and Brazil. If you enrol with KDP Select you cannot opt out of Kindle Unlimited.

Kindle Owners' Lending Library (KOLL)

Amazon Prime Members have access to books that are enrolled on the Kindle Owners' Lending Library. They can select one book each month to read for free. Amazon Prime members that have downloaded your book from the Lending Library cannot then lend your book to anyone else. Once that book is read it is returned to Amazon just like you would at a normal library. Authors receive a royalty for their book from the KDP Select Global Fund. If a Prime member wants to read your book again they can download it another month but you will not receive your royalty again. Readers can keep your book for as long as they want, until it is read and returned.

If you decide to enrol on KDP Select your book will automatically be available to the Kindle Owners' Lending Library which is currently only available in the US, UK, Germany, France and Japan. If you enrol with KDP Select you cannot opt out of the Kindle Owners' Lending Library.

You will receive a royalty payment from the KDP Select Global Fund when any Prime Member downloads your book.

When you look at your book in the Amazon store, you will notice two prices for your Kindle book, one which is the normal price, but the other will say it is free to Amazon Prime Members.

Price

$0.00 *Prime* (read for free, Join Amazon Prime)
$4.09 to buy

$24.16 *Prime*

KDP Select Global Fund

The KDP Select Global fund is set by Amazon every month. Participating authors are emailed informing them what the monthly fund will be. Each borrow through the Kindle Owners' Lending Library as well as each title read through the Kindle Unlimited scheme entitles you to a proportion of the fund. The amount you are paid from the fund for each borrow or read is dependent on many things. What Amazon set the Global fund at depends on the number of subscribers they have to Amazon Prime and Kindle Unlimited for the month. In March 2015 the global fund was set at $9.3 Million. To work out how much you would get per download depends on the total number of downloads of every book participating in the Kindle Owners Lending Library and Kindle Unlimited during that month. For example, if there were a total of five million downloads in March, you could expect to get just less than $2 per download ($9.3 million fund divided by 5 million downloads). You will only know exactly how much you have earned for books that have been borrowed on downloaded through Kindle Unlimited when you look at your royalty statements. For some authors, earning less than $2 in royalties is less than they would have earned if it was a normal sale, but for those books that sell for $0.99 a $2 royalty is a great bonus. Kindle Unlimited will also give you more exposure to impulse buys as readers don't take the cost of books into consideration. All of this you need to weigh up when considering whether to be part of KDP Select of not.

KDP Select All-Stars

In an attempt to reward writers and books that sell well through KDP Select, Amazon have created the KDP Select All-Stars - a chart that rewards the most read authors and most read titles each month. Winners each receive a financial bonus depending on their ranking which is calculated by combining the total number of books sold, plus the number of borrows from Kindle Unlimited and the Kindle Owners Lending Library during one month. Countdown Deals and Free Book Deals do not count towards the total number of books sold and will not effect your All-Star Ranking.

Currently, only authors and books sold in the US, UK and Germany are eligible for the KDP Select All-Stars.

The bonuses awarded in different countries are as follows:

ALL-STAR BONUSES - AMAZON.COM

Author Ranking	All-Star Bonus		Title Ranking	All-Star Bonus
1 - 10	$25,000		1 - 10	$2,500
11 - 20	$10,000		11 - 50	$1,000
21 - 30	$5,000		51 - 100	$500
31 - 50	$2,500			
51 - 100	$1,000			

ALL-STAR BONUSES - AMAZON.CO.UK

Author Ranking	All-Star Bonus		Title Ranking	All-Star Bonus
1 - 10	£2,000		1 - 10	£500
11 - 20	£1,500		11 - 50	£250
21 - 30	£750		51 - 100	£100
31 - 100	£500			

ALL-STAR BONUSES - AMAZON.DE

Author Ranking	All-Star Bonus	Title Ranking	All-Star Bonus
1 - 10	€7,500	1 - 10	€750
11 - 20	€5,000	11 - 50	€500
21 - 30	€3,500	51 - 100	€250
31 - 50	€2,500		
51 - 100	€1,500		
101 - 150	€500		

Free Book Deal

As part of your 90 day enrolment in KDP Select you are entitled to offer your book for free for up to five days during each 90 day period. You can pick when your promotion will start, use all five days up in one go or spread them out as you desire. The promotion day starts immediately after midnight Pacific Standard Time and ends at midnight Pacific Standard Time. You can schedule the promotion 24 hours before you wish it to start and can stop it during the promotional period if you wish. Your book will be listed in the free Bestseller list, which is separate to the normal Bestseller list but will revert back to the paid ranking system once your promotion has finished.

You will not be paid royalties on downloads for a book that is participating in a free promotional deal. The number of free books will appear on your sales dashboard alongside your sales and borrows.

During your 90 day enrolment you cannot schedule a Free Book Deal as well as a Kindle Countdown Deal, it has to be one or the other. You cannot accumulate your unused free promotional days and roll them over to another 90 day period.

Free periods boost awareness of your book and will result in many more downloads than if it were a paid book. Each free download does have significance on your ranking when you return to the normal paid Bestseller list, but the weight of it compared with a normal paid sale is much less. Because of the increased number of people downloading your book during a free period, you are also more likely to pick up a few reviews which helps long term by increasing buyer confidence.

There are many places you can promote your free book deal to increase awareness. Go to Appendix F to find 49 Free Websites That Will Promote Your Free Book.

Kindle Countdown Deals

Participation in this deal allows you to offer your book to readers for a time limited promotion at different price points, gradually increasing back to its original list price, potentially presenting your book to a larger audience. This deal is only available on books that are for sale on the US and UK Amazon sites, although authors in other countries can still implement the deal, but it will only be seen on Amazon in the US and UK. Other countries will not see the deal and your book will continue to be available at the regular local price.

Any book that is enrolled on the KDP Select scheme is eligible to participate in a Countdown Deal as long as the original list price is between $2.99 - $24.99 (amazon.com) and £1.93 - £14.99 (amazon.co.uk). It must also have been enrolled in KDP Select for more than 30 days prior to the start of the Countdown Deal. The promotional price must be discounted by $1 (or £1) or more, than the regular list price.

As time ticks away, your book jumps in increments back towards its regular price. For example, if you run a promotion that starts at $1.99, you could increase the price by $1 every two days until it hits its regular price of $3.99. The length of that countdown deal would be a total of four days. The maximum duration of a deal is seven days with a maximum number of price increments of five. The minimum time increment is one hour. You can schedule your Countdown Deal to start whenever you want, but it cannot be earlier than the beginning of the next full day after 24 hours from the time you arrange it.

You cannot run a Free Book Promotion as well as a Kindle Countdown Deal during the same 90 day KDP Select enrolment period. The regular price of your book must not change thirty days before the deal and fourteen days after the promotion finishes. Once the promotion has started you cannot stop it. The lowest price you can start your Countdown Deal is $0.99 (amazon.com) or £0.99 (amazon.co.uk).

Royalties are paid at the percentage that was chosen for the original price. For example if you are receiving 70% royalties on the regular price, you will still receive 70% of the promotional price even if it is below the threshold that would normally mean you would have to accept 35% royalties.

Amazon have a dedicated page where buyers can see all the books that are currently participating in a Countdown deal, separated into categories.

When you participate in a Kindle Countdown Deal buyers will see the promotional price as well as a countdown clock displaying the length of time buyers have to take advantage of the deal and what it will go up to once the time has run out.

Kindle Countdown Deal
Price goes up to £1.99 in
1 day, 12:34:07

As well as your normal monthly sales report you will be able to see a new report that indicates the sales performance and royalty earned at each promotional price point in the "Promotions" section of your sales report page.

How To Schedule A Kindle Countdown Deal Or Free Book Promotion

Go to your KDP Bookshelf and select the book you wish to arrange the deal for. On the Book Details Page you will see two options beneath a message that confirms you are enrolled in KDP Select.

(i) **This book is enrolled in KDP Select.**
Enrollment Details | Promote and Advertise

Click on "Promote and Advertise". You will then be taken to a new page where you can choose which price promotion you want to schedule.

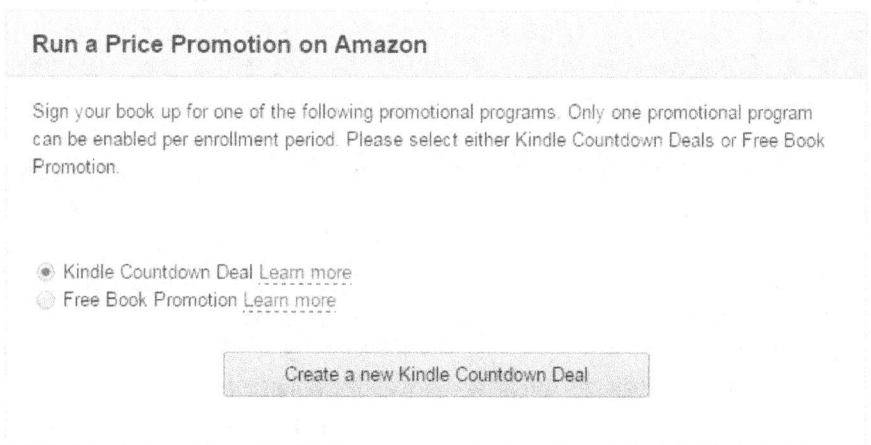

Tools to promote your book on Amazon

Run a Price Promotion on Amazon

Sign your book up for one of the following promotional programs. Only one promotional program can be enabled per enrollment period. Please select either Kindle Countdown Deals or Free Book Promotion.

⦿ Kindle Countdown Deal Learn more
○ Free Book Promotion Learn more

Create a new Kindle Countdown Deal

Select the promotion you want to schedule and click the yellow box.

For Kindle Countdown Deals:

Select Kindle Countdown Deals in the box and click "Create a new Kindle Countdown Deal for this book". This will take you to a new page where you can input the details for your deal.

Create a new Kindle Countdown Deal

1. Select marketplace.

Kindle Countdown Deals are configured by marketplace. You can schedule one Kindle Countdown Deal in each available marketplace during your current KDP Select term.

Marketplace: Amazon.co.uk ⇕

2. Choose when the promotion will start and end.

Kindle Countdown Deal promotions can run for up to 7 days.

Must be after January 16, 2015 (Why?)   Must be before February 4, 2015 (Why?)

Start: January 16, 2015   8:00 AM ⇕ GMT   End: 8:00 AM ⇕ GMT

3. Select the number of price increments for this promotion and the starting price. You will be able to view and edit your promotion schedule after clicking "Continue" below.

Number of price increments: 1 ⇕   Starting list price: £ 0.99 ⇕ *   Ending list price: £2.54 (original list price)

(What's this?)   (What's this?)

1. Select Marketplace. Your book can only be available as a Countdown Deal to Amazon customers in the US and UK. Select which location you would like this deal to be made available. If you want to run a Countdown Deal on both websites you will need to go back and set up a second deal in the other country once you have completed this one.

2. Choose When The Promotion Will Start And End. Countdown Deals are limited to 7 days in each country and they do not have to run at the same time. Choose the time and date you want the deal to begin and end.

3. Select Price Increments. Choose what you want the promotional price to start at, followed by the number of increments the deal will be divided into until it reaches the original price which will be displayed beside the "Ending list price". Depending on the list price you may find that the starting price and number of increments will be limited.

Once you click "Continue" you will see a fourth section open up confirming times and dates as well as price increments and duration. If you are happy with it click "Add Promotion" or alter dates, prices and increments until you've set it up the way you want.

4. Review promotion schedule

Below is an optional set of prices and start times for your promotion. Click on a price or increment to edit. Or, if you are happy with the prices and times, click **Add Promotion** below. Note that you will be able to edit your promotion up to 24 hours before it starts.

Increment		Duration	Price*	% Discount
1	January 19, 2015 at 8:00 AM (GMT)	36h	£0.99	62%
2	January 20, 2015 at 8:00 PM (GMT)	36h	£1.99	22%
End	January 22, 2015 at 8:00 AM (GMT)		Original list price £2.54	

* The promotional list price you provide is VAT-INCLUSIVE

Cancel   Add Promotion

For a Free Book Promotion:

Select Free Book Promotion in the box and click "Create a new Free Book Promotion Deal for this book". This will take you to a new page where you can input the dates you want your deal to run.

Create a new Free Book Deal

Choose when the promotion will start and end

Kindle Free Book Deal promotions can run for up to 5 days.

Start Date: [ ]   End Date: [ ]   Free promotion days used: 0 / 5

Open the calendars and choose when you want your deal to start and end. You are limited to a total number of five days during every 90 day period that the book is enrolled in KDP Select. Days do not need to be taken together, you could schedule one day one week, another the next etc, up to a total of five days. When you are done click "Save Changes". Whereas a Countdown Deal is limited to US and UK Amazon stores, the Free Book Deal is available on all marketplaces.

SHORTCUT - you can also manage your Free Book Deals and Countdown Deals directly from your KDP Bookshelf. Look for the book you wish to apply a deal to, then follow that row across the page until you see a column headed KDP Select with the option "Promote and Advertise" for the book. Click here to arrange a deal.

KDP Select
Learn more

> Promote and
Advertise
> Info

If you are using the new version "Bookshelf", select the options box on the far right beside the relevant book and in the opening window select "Promote and Advertise".

Edit Details

Edit Rights, Royalty, and Pricing

KDP Select Info

Promote and Advertise

Edit Matchbook

Unpublish

3. Preparing The Inside Of Your Book

Once you have finished writing your book, had it edited and formatted, you are nearly ready to start uploading it to KDP. But there are a few important pieces of information you need to add to your book and prepare it for uploading.

Front Matter

When your book is available to Amazon customers, they will have the option of being able to read 10% of it to sample your writing and see if they want to buy the book. It is important to make the most of this facility and really sell the book.

Before the main content of your book place some highlighted reviews that you might already have. This helps to convince a potential reader that they need to find out why your book is so great. It is also a good idea to include live links to Amazon pages of other books you might have written, together with a link to your website so they can find out more about you.

After this it is a good idea to include a copyright page, attributing the rights of the book to yourself or anyone else that was involved in creating the content.

Kindle books also need to have a "Contents" page at the front of the book with each chapter linked to the relevant chapter inside the book. This makes it easier for readers to navigate to different chapters.

Acceptable File Formats

You can upload your book in various formats including word, html, mobi, epub, rich text format, plain text, or pdf.

The maximum file size is 650MB. Images need to be a maximum of 5MB to make conversion quicker and more likely to be successful. To reduce your book size, upload images in jpeg format and compress them to 50-60%. You can also decrease the quality of the image by reducing the dots per inch (dpi).

The two easiest formats for authors to upload a book to KDP are in Word and Mobi - both require no html coding skills and are quick to transfer.

Microsoft Word

Word is the most widely used word processing software. Once your book is completed you can upload your finished file directly to your Book Details Page.

However, if your book contains images you will need to convert the word document into a web page before you can upload.

It's a pretty straight forward process:

1. Create a zipped folder and title it with your book name.

2. Open the word file that contains the internal content of your book.

3. Save your word book as "Web Page".

4. You will notice that a html file has now been created, together with another folder entitled [YOUR BOOK]_files which contains all of the images inside your book.

5. Drag and drop the html file and the image folder into the zipped folder.

6. Upload the zip folder to KDP

Mobi Format

One of the best ways to upload your book is by converting it into a mobi file, which is the file type Amazon uses for Kindle books. The advantage of doing it this way is so that you can see what the finished book will look like before you even begin to upload it to the internet. This is also the easiest way to create a file if your book contains any images.

To convert to mobi:

1. First download the Kindle Previewer from Amazon's Tools and Resources page (https://kdp.amazon.com/help?topicId=A3IWA2TQYMZ5J6) to your computer.

Kindle Previewer v2.94 for Windows (7 and above)   Download Now

Kindle Previewer v2.94 for Intel Mac (OSX 10.7 and above)   Download Now

2. Save the word file of your book as a "Web Page". This is a html file.

3. Open Kindle Previewer and open the "Web page" version of your book.

4. Kindle Previewer will automatically construct the mobi file, including images inside the book and open a new folder in the same place the original "Web Page" was saved. The new folder will be titled "converted-[YOUR BOOKS NAME]". Double click this folder and you will see the mobi file inside.

5. With Kindle Previewer still open you will be able to look at each page of your book as it will appear on various different devices.

6. Upload the mobi file to the Book Details Page.

4. Kindle Kids' Book Creator

Kindle Kids' Book Creator is an easy way to create picture books for Kindle that can be displayed with two pages side by side, just like you would see with a normal children's picture book. You can create the book offline, save as a mobi file and upload directly to your KDP Book Details Page like you would with a normal book. You can also make text pop ups so that it is easier to read.

The files you upload into Kids' Book Creator can be jpeg, pdf, tiff, png or ppm formats. Books created in this way can only be read on Kindle Fire tablets, the Fire phone, as well as iPhone and Android Apps.

The maximum file size is limited to 650MB

To begin, download the relevant version of Kids Book Creator from Amazon's Tools and Resources page (https://kdp.amazon.com/help?topicId=A3IWA2TQYMZ5J6) to your computer.

Kindle Kids Book Creator v1.0 for Windows (7, 8)

Kindle Kids Book Creator v1.0 for Intel Mac (OSX 10.7 and above)

Once installed you can import the images you want, reposition the sequence and add text to create your children's picture book.

How To Build A Children's Picture Book

1. Open the Kindle Kids' Book Creator. You will be given the option of either opening an existing book, or create a new Kids' book. Click on new book.

2. The following window gives you information on how to use the Kids' Book Creator. Click "Continue" to begin.

3. You now need to provide details of your book. Enter the Title, Author and Publisher, together with the language of the book.

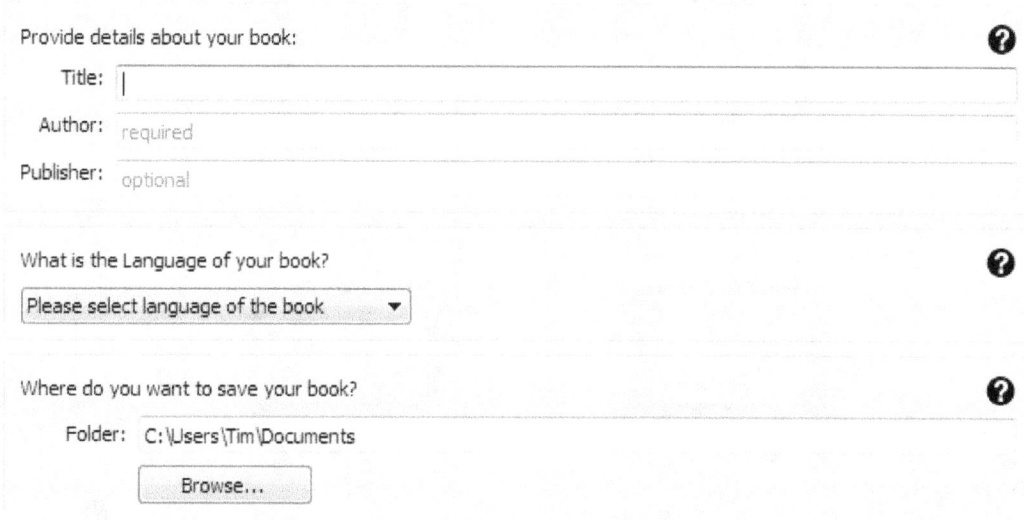

The folder on your computer where you intend to save your book needs to be empty. If you don't have one, go back and create one using the book name as the folder name so you can easily recognise it.

4. You will now need to start thinking about how you want your book to look. Landscape gives the reader the opportunity to see two pages side by side (one picture, one text, or two pictures, or one wide picture), whereas portrait allows only one image on the screen at a time. If you choose portrait you can then click through to the next stage. If you choose landscape you will also need to decide whether to have one or two pages on screen at a time, as well as where you want your first page to appear. The first page inside your book is not the book cover. That is added separately. When you have made your choices click "Continue".

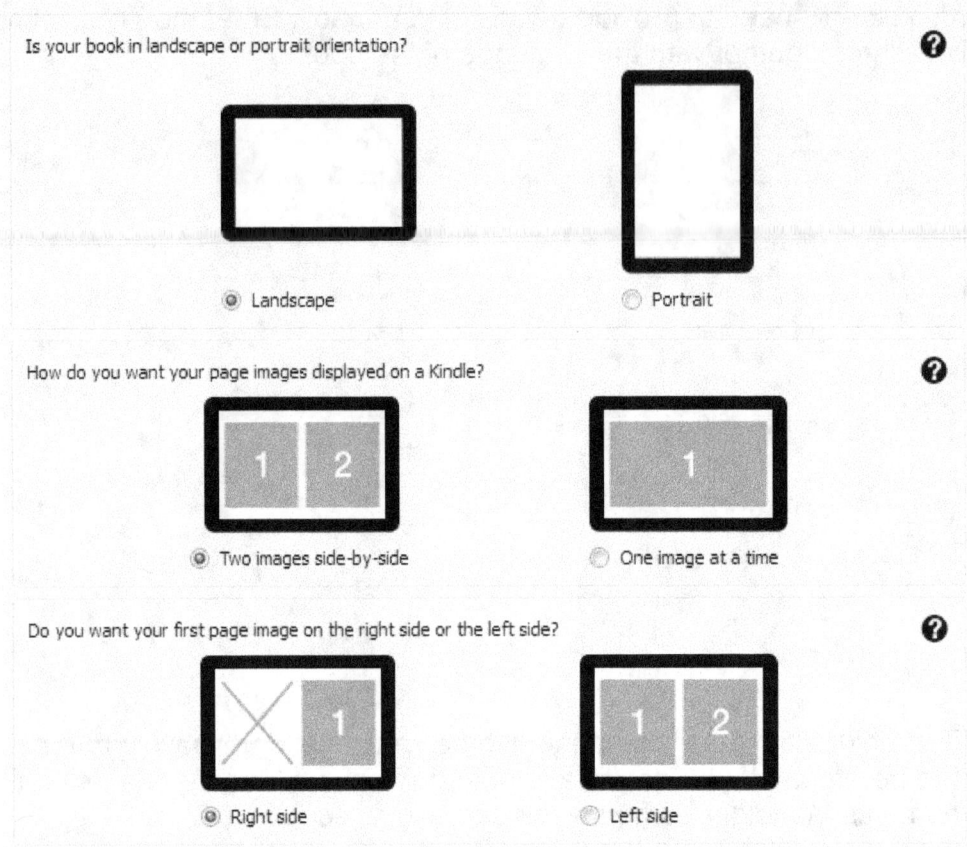

5. Now it is time to either upload the whole book if you have it ready in pdf format, or upload just the cover. If you only import the cover at this stage you will then need to upload each individual page to create your book.

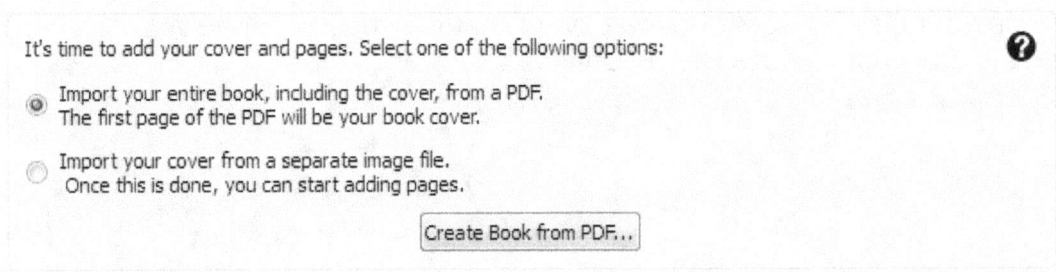

You will now be taken through to the part of the software where you can build the content inside your book. If you uploaded a pdf file each page will already be displayed in the sequence of the original file. If you uploaded just the cover all of the internal pages will be empty ready for you to fill.

Adding pages

Add an image to a page by clicking the "Add page" button.

This will open up a window where you can select the image from your computer. Once you start adding more pages you will see an option appear, asking where you want the new page to be added. The options are:

- Add Page At The Beginning of the Book

- Add Page At The End of the Book

- Add Page Before Page [Select Number]

- Add Page After Page [Select Number]

- Add Page Between the Two Sides of Page [Select Number]

Try and add pages in a sequential manner. If you want two pictures side by side, select the "Add Page Between the Two Sides of Page [Select Number]".

Deleting Pages

Make sure you have selected the page you wish to delete before you click on the "Delete page" button.

This will open up a window where you can choose what you want to delete.
The options are:

- Both Sides

- The Left Side Only

- The Right Side Only

Changing Book Settings

Click on the "Book Settings" button then select "Metadata". This will open the choices you made when you were setting up your Kids' Book. You can also change the cover image here if you wish too.

Adding Text

If you want to add text somewhere on the screen, click the "Add Text" button. You will see a text box appear that can be moved around the screen and positioned where you wish, including over the top of images. The box can be manipulated into the size you desire. Once you are happy with the rough size and position, click inside the box and type the words you want to see.

You can change the appearance of the text by using one of the toolbar options.

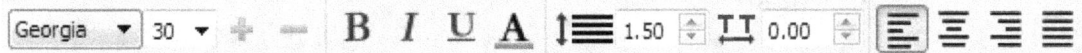

In order from left to right:

- Font style (No other option available except Georgia unless you upload more fonts)

- Font Size

- Increase or decrease the size of the text with the + and - symbols

- Bold text

- Italic text

- Underline text

- Text colour

- Line spacing

- Spread between letters

- Left align

- Centre align

- Right align

- Justified

Once you have added text you will see that a button appears above the text box:

💬 View Pop-up

The text box you have created is a clickable area on the readers Kindle that allows the text you have just written to appear in a larger size above the book page so that readers can see the text more clearly. This is especially useful if you have small sized text in little sections amongst the images. When the reader taps somewhere else on the screen the pop up disappears. To add text for the pop up, just click on the "View Pop-up" button. You will see that it automatically has the same text in it that you had previously written, but if you want to type different text in here you can do so by clicking the "Unlink from Page Text" button and typing in the pop up text.

Adding additional Fonts

The standard font on Kids' Book Creator is Georgia, but you can embed additional fonts to make it consistent with the text readers are seeing on the page.

To embed a font, go to "Tools" and select "Add Font". The font files you can embed are ttf and otf formats. You can only embed the fonts if you have the original files on your computer. When you have embedded the font you will see it as a selectable option in the "Font Style" box in the Text Toolbar.

Saving and Publishing

When you have uploaded everything to the Kids' Book Creator, make sure you save it by going to "File" and "Save". This will save the book in the folder you created earlier. This has saved your project, but not created the mobi file that you will need to upload to your KDP Book Details Page.

It is important to preview what you've done so you can see how it might look when someone is reading your book on their Kindle. To do this click on "Book Preview" on the menu bar. The software will convert your book into mobi format and open Kindle Previewer where you will be able to see what it looks like on different Kindle Fire devices.

Once you are happy and ready to publish go to "File" and click "Save For Publishing". A mobi version of your book will be created and saved in the folder you created at the beginning of this process. This is the file you need to upload to section six of the KDP Book Details Page.

5. Kindle Textbook Creator

Textbook Creator is a downloadable piece of software that allows you to produce Kindle books that have a lot of charts, graphs and equations - formatted segments of eBooks that don't typically translate well when converting your book from word to mobi. Textbook creator builds your book outside of KDP to create a Kindle Package Format file. You can also include audio, video and image pop-ups - features that are not available with a normal mobi file. The benefit of using Textbook Creator is that it preserves the size and layout of books which contain a lot of text and images. How your pages look in a pdf file will be exactly how they get translated into your Kindle Textbook and how the end user will see them. This means that you can align pictures within text, break up the page with columns and even import tables. As the book is a fixed format eBook, the font size is also fixed on the end users device. You will therefore need to carefully consider the size of your font in the pdf file before converting. The big downside to Textbooks is that you cannot include any hyperlinks, and it is only readable on certain devices that support audio and visual such as Fire devices, Android and iPhones.

But, there are also additional features that make reading a Textbook a more interactive experience, including:

- Multi-coloured highlighting

- Notebook - students can make their own notes and capture key text and images

- Flashcards - students can create flashcards to help when they are studying

- Dictionary - discover definitions

- Pinch and zoom - readers can zoom into the page by up to 400%

Authors creating Textbooks can earn the 35% or 70% royalty options and enroll their books in KDP Select just like a normal Kindle book.

Because there are features in a Textbook that are different to a normal eBook, it is a good idea to provide some sort of guide at the beginning of your book that explains to the reader they can click on image, audio or movie icons to find out more information. There should also be some basic instructions advising the reader that they can pinch and zoon into each page if they want a closer look.

Download Kindle Textbook Creator

To begin, download the relevant version of Kindle Textbook Creator into your computer by going to the KDP Tools and Resources page (https://kdp.amazon.com/help?topicId=A3IWA2TQYMZ5J6).

When you first open the software you will be given the choice to either "Open an Existing Book" if you are already working on a project, or "Create New Textbook from File".

Creating A New Textbook

The easiest and quickest way to create a textbook is to write the entire book as normal in a word processing program like Word, including all of the images you want. Do not add a table of contents in the word document but bookmark each chapter heading.

Once complete you will then need to convert it into a pdf file to import it into the Textbook Creator.

When your book is ready, open Textbook Creator, find the file on your computer and click "Open". Your entire book should now be displayed in front of you with each individual page on the left as thumbnails and a bigger view in the centre of the screen. You can change the size of the central viewing panel by zooming in or out from the "Zoom" option at the top left of your screen.

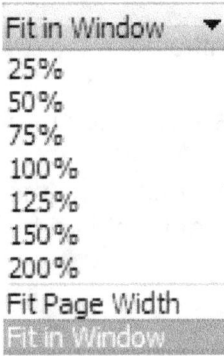

Adding A Page

Before importing more pages into your Textbook, you will need to select from the thumbnail pages where you want your imported pages to go. Select the page in the original document that will feature before the page you want to import. Click the blue "Insert" button and select the "Page(s) from PDF".

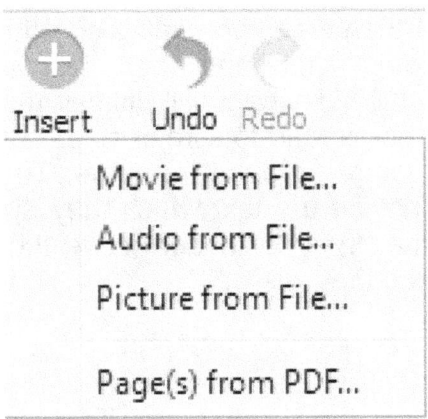

This will open a new window where you can find the page or pages on your computer. Click "Open" and the pages will be imported into your Textbook. All other pages will automatically become reordered and numbered.

Deleting a Page

Find the page you wish to remove from the Textbook from the thumbnail images and right click, then "Delete Selected Page". All other pages will automatically get reordered and numbered.

Reordering Pages

You can change the position of any page by clicking and dragging the thumbnail page image to a new position.

Adding Images

It is advisable to create the complete document, including images before importing it into the Textbook Creator. However, you can include additional images in the document that are clickable so they expand to full screen size. Image files need to be in jpeg or png format.

First, select the page where you want to insert the image to from the thumbnails on the left. Click "Insert" and select "Picture from file" and find the image you wish to use from your computer. You can now click anywhere on that page to drop an image icon.

On the right side of the screen you can also add some commentary to go with the image including a title and short description. When someone clicks the image icon on their device it will display the image, together with the title and description and expand to screen size. You can move the image icon by clicking and dragging it around the page. The best place for these icons is in the margins, beside the text which they apply to. You could use them beside images in the page so readers have the option to enlarge the image to get a closer look if they wish.

Adding Videos

You can import .mp4 video files into your Textbook.

First, select the page you want to insert the video to from the thumbnails on the left. Click "Insert" and select "Movie from file" and find the file you wish to use from your computer. You can now click anywhere on that page to drop a movie icon.

On the right side of the screen you can also add some commentary to go with the video including a title and short description. When someone clicks the movie icon on their device it will display the video, together with the title and description. You can move the movie icon by clicking and dragging it around the page. The best place for these icons is in the margins, beside the text which they apply to.

Adding Audio

You can import .mp3 audio files into your Textbook.

First, select the page you want to insert the audio to from the thumbnails on the left. Click "Insert" and select "Audio from file" and find the file you wish to use from your computer. You can now click anywhere on that page to drop an audio icon.

On the right side of the screen you can also add some commentary to go with the audio including a Title and short description. When someone clicks the audio icon on their device it will display the title and description together with a Play button. You can move the audio icon by clicking and dragging it around the page. The best place for these icons is in the margins, beside the text which they apply to.

Creating A Table of Contents

There are two ways of doing this - automatically or manually.

If you bookmarked every chapter heading in your word document and preserved them in the pdf file, Textbook Creator will have automatically recognised the chapter headings and created your table of contents for you.

If the bookmarks didn't transfer into the pdf you will need to add the chapters in manually. Find the page of your first chapter in the thumbnails. Click it to view in the main viewing area. On the right of the screen you will see a header called "Page Properties". Click the box that says "Include Page in Table of Contents" and type the chapter title in the box. You are limited to 100 characters. To make it ordered and structured, don't forget to include the chapter number.

Page Properties	
☑ Include Page in Table of Contents	
Page Title	14/100
1 Introduction	

Do this for all of the chapters. When the book is finished, the Textbook Creator will create a separate contents table for you that goes with the book.

You can see if a certain page is marked as a new chapter by the blue triangle in the top left corner of the thumbnail pages.

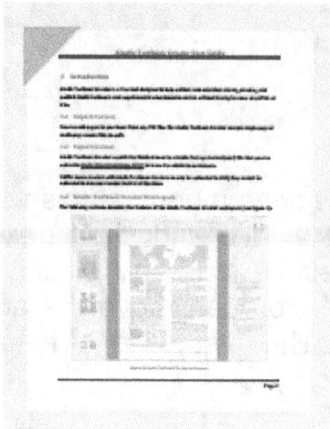

Previewing Your Book

Click the "Preview" button in the top right of the screen.

This then opens two windows. A large one which shows you what your book will look like on various devices. You can choose to view it on a Fire HDX 8.9, Fire HDX, Fire Phone, iPhone, iPad, Android Phone, and Android Tablet. Towards the bottom of the Inspector box you will see arrows pointing left and right - these move your pages forward or backwards. At the bottom of the Inspector box you can see the tab for the Table of contents.

Check that each chapter has been included and the headings are spelt correctly.

Close the previewer when you have finished by clicking the large X in the right corner.

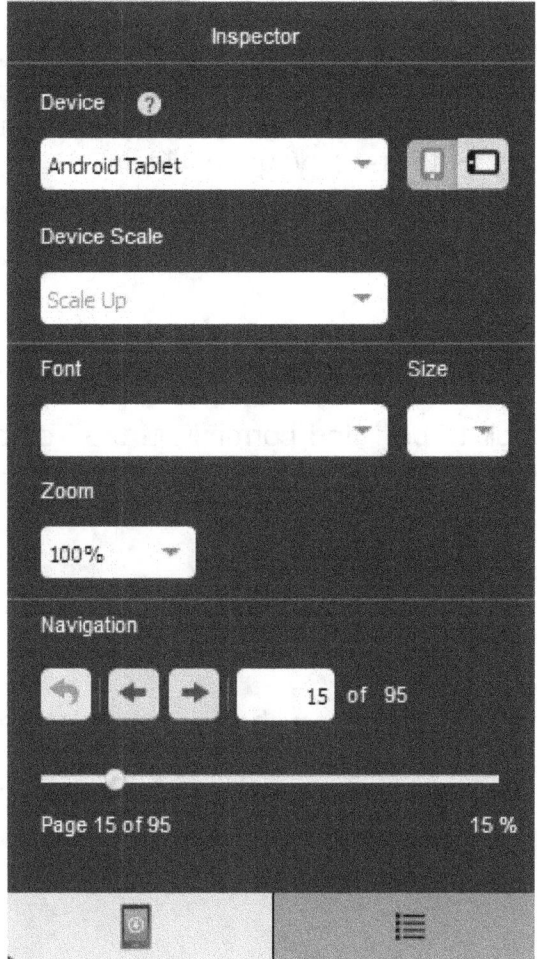

Saving And Exporting Your Textbook

Make sure that you regularly save the progress on your book as there is not currently an automatic save facility built into the software.

Go to "File" and "Save Book As". This will save your project as a kcb file, together with a folder containing the resources (images and videos). The kcb file is not the one you want to upload to your KDP account. For this you will need to create a "Package" file - kpf file. Go to "File" and click "Package for Publishing" or click the "Package" button in the top right of the screen.

Select where you want to save the file and click "Save". There is a maximum file size of 650MB allowed for a kpf file. If your book is greater than this you will not be able to upload it to KDP. Reduce the size of images and videos in the software you originally used when creating the pdf file then upload to Textbook creator to create your kpf file.

When you open your KDP account, add the kpf file in section 6 (Upload Your Book File) in the Book Details Page.

Making Your Book Appear In The Textbook Category On Amazon

For your Textbook to be listed correctly in the Textbook Category on amazon.com you will need to use the following piece of text as one of your keyword phrases:

kdp_textbook_submission

This keyword phrase (together with underscores) needs to be included in the Keyword options in section 3 Target Your Book to Customers in the KDP Book Details Page. This only applies to Textbooks in the US Amazon store.

6. Kindle Comic Creator

You can convert your comics and graphic novels into a Kindle eBook by using the Kindle Comic Creator. As most comics are illustrated using different panels to tell the story, Kindle Comic Creator identifies the panels and allows the user to select each panel, resulting in its expansion to fill the screen and deliver an easier reading experience.

Your comic book will need to be set out in clear panels to work on a Kindle.

File types accepted include jpeg, png, pdf, tiff or ppm. You can set up your book to show a single or double page spread. Comics can only be read on Kindle Fire HD, Kindle Fire HD 8.9, Kindle Fire, Kindle Paperwhite, Kindle Keyboard, Kindle for iPad, iPhone and Kindle Android apps.

Download Kindle Comic Creator

To begin, download the relevant version of Kindle Comic Creator into your computer by going to the KDP Tools and Resources page (https://kdp.amazon.com/help?topicId=A3IWA2TQYMZ5J6.

When you first open the software you will be given the choice to either "Open an Existing Book" if you are already working on a project, or "Create New Textbook from File".

Open an existing Book

Create a New Book

Create A New Book

As soon as you begin a new book you will be given several set up options. Begin by selecting the language your book is written in.

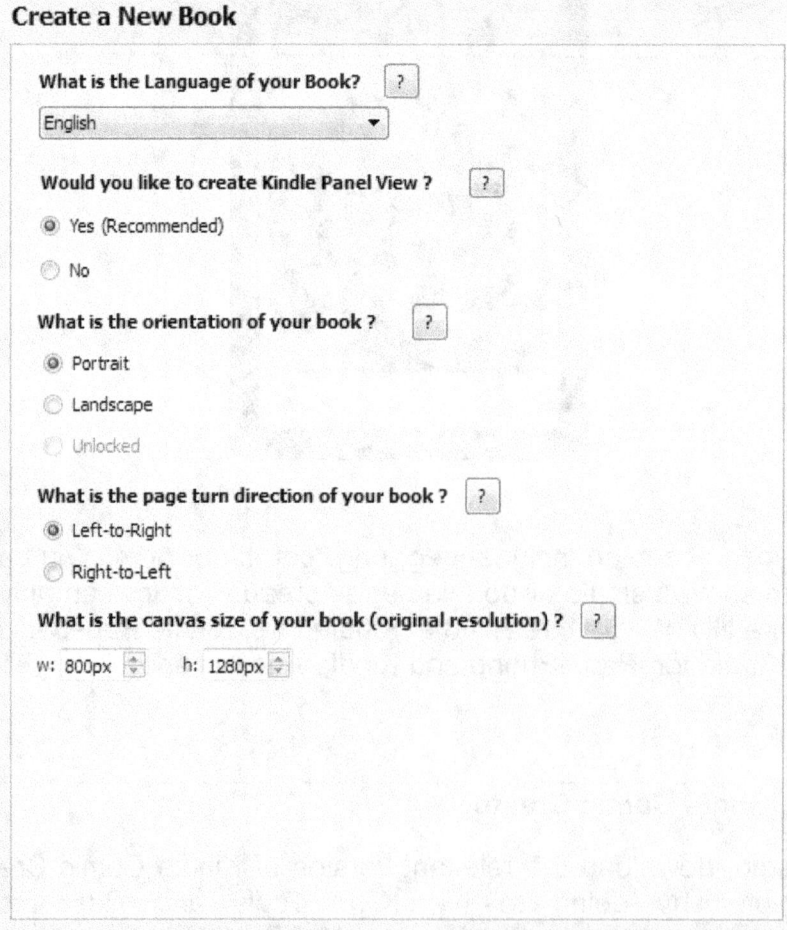

The second question is about Kindle Panel View - this is where the reader can tap the screen to enlarge part of an image or text to read more easily. Select "Yes" and move on to the next option - page orientation. If you choose portrait, the reader will see one page at a time. If you want to create a comic that is landscape with two pages side by side, you will need to answer "No" to Kindle Panel View and set orientation to "Unlocked". Next choose the way the pages turn. This will depend on the language the user will be reading it in. You then need to define the size of the page images. For portrait the default size is 800px x 1280px but you can change these sizes if you need to. Click "Continue" to move to your Metadata. Enter the title, author's name and publisher (if you have one) and upload the cover image. The project will need to be saved in an empty folder, so make sure you have one ready for your files to be saved to.

Once you are ready click "Start Adding Pages". A new window will automatically open. You can either add the first image file of your comic, or if you have the complete comic already created in a pdf file, you can open it and all the pages will be imported into Comic Creator.

Screen Layout

You will now be taken through to the part of the software where you can build the content inside your comic. The screen is laid out with the "Book Manager" panel on the left where each individual page is shown as a thumbnail, whilst the main "Design" panel shows the currently selected page in a bigger view in the centre of the screen. You can change the size of the "Design" panel by zooming in or out from the option in the toolbar.

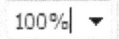

If you cannot see the zoom option in the toolbar, go to "View" then "Toolbars" then "Comic Toolbars".

Adding Pages

Add a page by clicking the "Add page" button in the "Book Manager" panel.

This will open up a window where you can select the image or pdf file from your computer. Each new page that you add will appear immediately after the selected thumbnail on the left of the screen.

To import a section from an image or pdf file, click the arrow beside "Add Page" and select "Add Custom Pages". Find the file on your computer and click open to see it in a separate window. Right click on the image and select "New Page" to see a blue outlined box. Adjust the size of it to select the area of the page you want to import into your project. If there is another section of the image you want to add to your comic, right click again to create another box and select the area. When you are done click on "OK" and each selected panel will be created as new pages in your comic.

Deleting Pages

Make sure you have selected the page you wish to delete before you click on the "Delete page" button.

Rearranging Your Pages

You can change the page order by dragging and dropping the page thumbnails into the desired location in the "Page Manager" panel.

Naming Your Pages

Go to the Page Toolbar at the top of the page.

Select a page from your thumbnails in the "Page Manager" then type in the name of the page (Introduction/chapter 1, etc.) and press return. The page will now be renamed from Page-1 to whatever you have typed. This is then used to create you contents table which appears on the readers device.

Changing Book Settings

Click on the "Book Settings" button then select "Metadata". This will open a new window with two tabs at the top. "Panels" will show the set up choices you made when you were setting up your Comic Book. Click "Metadata" to change the title, author, publisher and cover image. If you click the button "Advanced Settings". You can import a table of contents if you already have one created on your computer, but don't worry if you don't, a table of contents will automatically be generated with your comic when it gets converted to mobi format ready for uploading to KDP. Click "Kindle Panels" to change the border width and colour of the panels in your comic.

To Create A Panel

Kindle Comic Creator can automatically detect the panels you have created on your pages. Right click on the page you want to work on and click "Detect Panels" then "In This Page". Numbered boxes should show up around the panels on the page. Alternatively, you can manually create panels by right clicking on the chosen page and selecting "New Kindle Panel".

New Kindle Panel
New Text Panel
Detect Panels   >

A green bordered box will appear on your "Design" screen. Drag the bottom right corner and top left corners to position the panel over the area you want to make a clickable area. Right click in the panel to open up options:

Set Zoom Level
Delete Panel
Edit Panel
Show Panel

Click "Edit Panel". This will show you an enlarged version of the page where you can select what the reader will see when they click on the panel. This will be the area of the page that will enlarge on their device. It doesn't have to be the same area that you made clickable when you created the panel, but it usually is.

"Set Zoom Level". When a reader double clicks the panel it will expand. Select how much you want the panel to expand to from presets - 100%, 125%, 150% and 200% or select your own.

"Show Panel". This shows you what the reader will see when they click on the panel. The background becomes darker and the panel expands.

"Delete Panel" removes the panel.

Each panel on your page will be shown by a green bordered box and assigned a number then listed on the right side of the screen in a section called "Panel Manager".

To Create A Text Panel

Select the page you are working on and right click and select "New Text Panel".

New Kindle Panel
New Text Panel
Detect Panels   >

A green bordered box will appear on your "Design" screen. Drag the bottom right and top left corners to position the panel over the area you want to make clickable.

Double click the box to open a large box where you can type in the pop up text.

To alter the text go to "View" then "Toolbars" then "Rich Text Toolbar". The text toolbar will appear at the top of the page.

In order from left to right:

- Font Size

- Increase or decrease the size of the text with the + and - symbols

- Bold text

- Italic text

- Underline text

- Text colour

- Insert image

- Font Name - standard is Times New Roman unless you embed additional fonts

- Line Height - the distance between the lines

- Letter Spacing - the space between each letter

Adding Additional Fonts

The standard font on Comic Creator is Times New Roman, but you can embed additional fonts to make it consistent with the text readers are seeing on the page.

To embed a font, go to "Tools" and select "Add Embedded Font". The font files you can embed are ttf and otf formats. You can only embed the fonts if you have the original files on your computer. When you have embedded the font you will see it as a selectable option in the "Font Name" box in the Text Toolbar.

Do not let any panels overlap. You will see a yellow highlighted "Warning" message appear inside the panels that overlap.

Each panel is assigned a number and you will see them in the Panel Manager on the right side of the screen. You can change the order of the panels by dragging and dropping them into the positions you want. You can easily delete panels from the Panel Manager too.

Creating A Landscape Orientation Comic

If you want to create a comic that features two pages side by side, or one wide image that spans the width of the readers Kindle, you will need to set the comic up as follows:

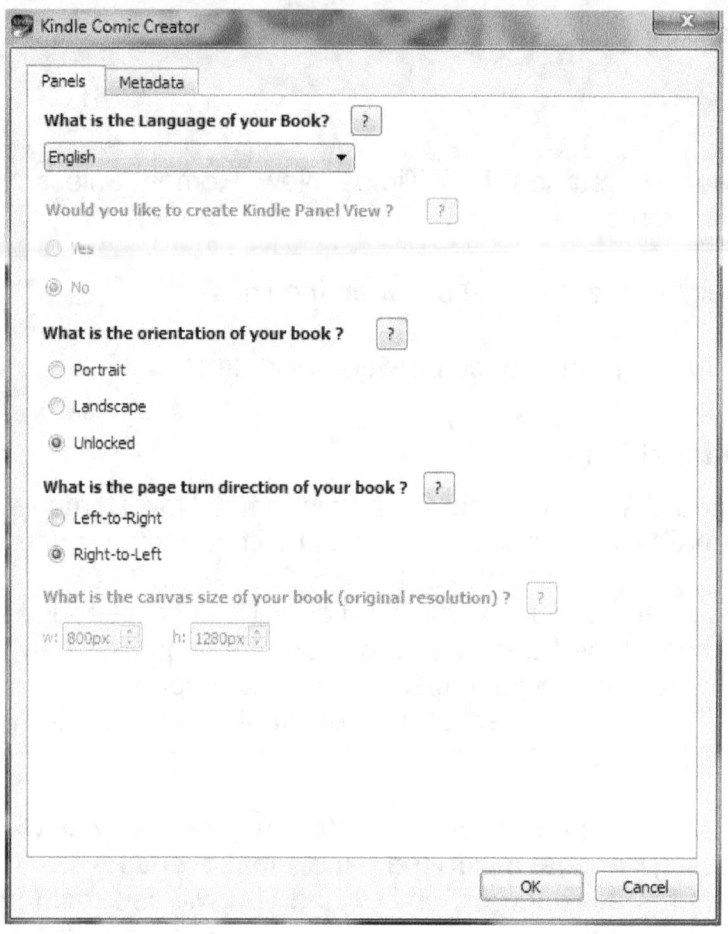

You can see that the Kindle Panel View is turned off and the orientation is set to "Unlock". Now, when you add a page you will have the option of being able to put two pages side by side or a double page spread. When you are arranging your pages you will have the additional option of changing your page settings. This button appears in the "Page Manager" panel.

Click this for more page options:

Double Page Spread

Facing Pages

Clear

Set All Double Page Spread

Set All Facing Pages

Clear All

Selecting "Facing Pages" will join two pages together with a narrow white line dividing them, whereas Double Page Spread is two pages joined seamlessly together. You can set these individually or for the entire comic.

Although this orientation looks a lot more like a traditional comic, you cannot use Kindle Panels with this set up so no images or text can be enlarged by tapping the screen. Readers will have to manually pinch and zoom to read text if it is small.

Saving Your Project

Periodically, it is a good idea to save your project. Go to "File" and "Save". This will save the book in the folder you created earlier. This has saved your project, but not created the mobi file that you will need to upload to your KDP Book Details Page.

Building And Previewing Your Book

Click "Build" then "Build and Preview". This will create a mobi file that can be uploaded to section six of the KDP Book Details Page. It will also open the comic in the Kindle Previewer program where you can view it as it would look on different Kindle devices.

7. Kindle Previewer

It is always a good idea to review the interior of your book before uploading and publishing to KDP. Amazon have created Kindle Previewer, a piece of free software that you can download into your computer. It allows you simulate what your book would look like on different devices. At present you are limited to viewing your book as it would be seen on a Kindle Voyage, Kindle DX, Kindle Fire HD, Kindle Fire HDX or a Kindle Fire HDX8.9", Kindle for iPad and iPhone

Don't forget that when it comes to uploading your book to KDP you will have the option to view a preview of your book online as you complete the Book Details Page.

Download Kindle Previewer

To begin, download the relevant version of Kindle Previewer into your computer by going to the KDP Tools and Resources page (https://kdp.amazon.com/help?topicId=A3IWA2TQYMZ5J6).

Opening A Book

When you open the Kindle Previewer software you will see the following window.

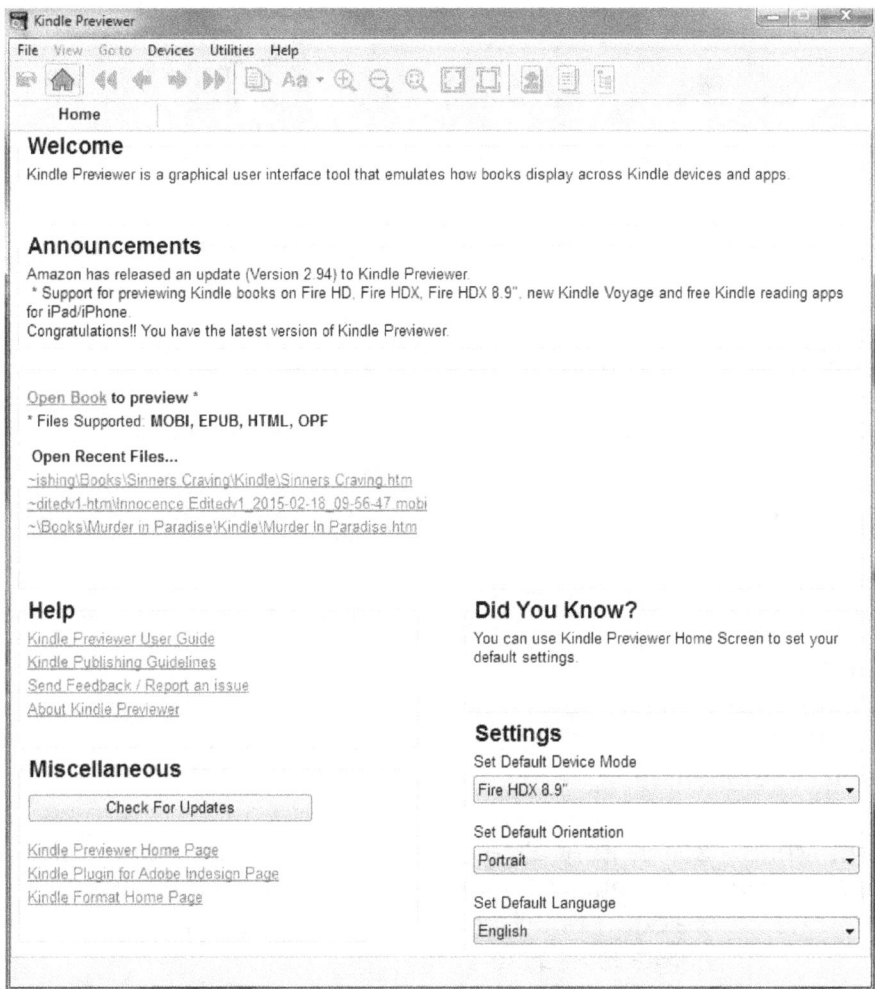

To open a book click "Open Book" and find it on your computer. You need to upload a mobi file to KDP for it to be read on a Kindle. Luckily Kindle Previewer will convert other files into mobi ready for upload. So, not only can you view your book, you can also convert it into the suggested file type. If you have been working in word to create your book, save it first as a web page (html document) then open in Kindle Previewer and it will be automatically converted into mobi format. This is particularly useful if you are incorporating images into the book. The alternative would be uploading a zip folder with all the files to KDP.

You can change the default settings for your Kindle Previewer by selecting alternative options in the three drop down menus in the bottom right of the Previewer home page. Change the Default Device, Orientation and language.

When you have opened your book you will see a screen that simulates the size of the selected reading device.

At the top of the Previewer you will see the following toolbar:

In order from left to right:

- Go back

- Home - back to the Welcome page of Previewer

- Back to previous section

- Back a page

- Forward a page

- Forward to next section

- Rotate Screen - you can view how the book would look if held in the landscape orientation

- Font Menu - select Font Size to increase or decrease the size of the font. (1 being the smallest)
  - select Font Face to change the font. Usually only Georgia is available
  - select Colour Mode. Normal (Black text on white background), Night (White text on black background), or Sepia (Brown text on cream background).

- Scale Down - decreases the size of the viewing window

- Scale Up - Increases the size of the viewing window

- Cover - view the cover

- Table of contents

- NCX View - this is a list of chapter headings, like a hyperlinked table of contents

Viewing On Different Devices

When you have opened your book, go to "Devices" at the top of the page.

- Click Kindle Ink to view in Kindle Voyage and Kindle DX

- Click Kindle Fire to view in Fire HD, HDX and HDX8.9"

- Click Kindle for iOS to view your book on iPad and iPhone. This requires a conversion to an azk file.

8. Preparing Your Cover

Every book needs a great cover and one that fits the genre expectations. This is the first thing that any potential reader will see. If it is poorly created, irrelevant to your target audience or made of low quality images, readers are never going to click through to your book product page to find out more. Everyone who dismisses the cover image is a lost sale, even if the inside is a work of literary genius. No one will ever know.

When considering your book cover, you need to make sure it follows the requirements set out by Amazon.

1. The book cover must be in jpeg or tiff format.

2. The image must be a minimum of 625 pixels on the shortest side and 1000 pixels on the longest side. For optimum quality you should aim to have your image 1562 pixels wide by 2500 pixels high

3. It needs to be saved with 72 dots per inch (dpi)

4. The file must also be no bigger than 50MB

5. Save the file in RGB colours, rather than CMYK

6. If your image has a white background put a thin gray border around it to distinguish it from the sales page background

You do not need to add your cover image to the word document that contains the contents of your book. During the publishing process you will get the opportunity to upload your book cover separately and the two will automatically be combined on the readers Kindle.

9. Cover Creator

If you haven't had the cover of your book designed for you, Amazon offer the services of their "Cover Creator" program to help you make your own. You can use an image of your own (make sure it is royalty free and has a model release if it contains humans) or one from their own gallery. They provide you with a variety of layouts and designs to choose from.

How To Create Your Cover

It is a good idea to prepare your cover before you are ready to publish. Go into your KDP account and click on "Add new title" to open up the Book Details Page for uploading a new book. You will see in section 5 that there is a button that says "Launch Cover Creator". Click this to design your cover.

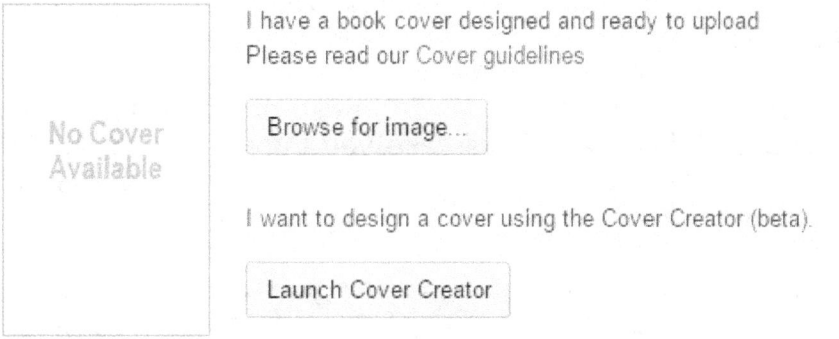

This will open a new window which shows you the three stages to create your cover. Click "Continue" to begin immediately.

Step 1. Choose Your Design

Begin by choosing an image. You can either browse through Amazon's gallery of images that you are allowed to use without paying royalties, or you can upload an image from your own computer. The third option is a "Placeholder Image". This is used when you have no cover image and just want to put something there as a temporary measure. This might be used in the case of a pre-order where no cover has been created yet.

From Image Gallery - If you decide to use one of Amazon's images click "From Image Gallery" and it will take you through to a gallery that is divided into categories. Search through the categories until you find the image you want then click "Use This Image" to go through to step 2.

From My Computer - By clicking on this you will open a window with your computer files listed. Select the image you want to use and click open. It will then upload to "Cover Creator" and take you through to step 2.

Step 2. Style & Edit

Once your image has been chosen you will see a page that shows different variations of the image, title, subtitle and author name. Some of the designs use the image, others do not. Hover over one of them to select that style.

You will then see an enlarged version of the cover you have chosen as well as three buttons beneath it.

The first button (left) will change the color of the background, accent and text. You can do this individually or by selecting a suggested color scheme.

The middle button shows different layouts for the text. There are various options as to where you might want to place it.

Click the third button (right) to change the font.

Step 3. Preview

When you are happy with the color, layout and font, click "Preview" where you will be able to see what your cover will look like in three different versions:

1. Color Mode - This shows how your cover will look on a color device

2. Grayscale Mode - This shows how your cover will look on a non-color device

3. Thumbnail Mode - This shows your cover reduced in size as it will look in an Amazon store

If you are happy click "Save & Submit" to add the cover to your KDP Book Details Page. The image will be added to this page. You can save it in draft for later if you are not ready to add in all of the other book details yet.

If you want to go back at any time and edit the cover you will see a button beside your cover in the Book Details Page. Click "Edit My Cover Creator Design" to be taken back into Cover Creator.

10. Creating A Great Product Description

If you have managed to get a reader to your book page, they are going to want to know what your book is about. This is the golden opportunity to sell your book. What you write and how the book sales page looks is essential to clinch the deal.

It is better to be organized and work on your book description before you are faced with an empty box in the KDP Book Details Page which might result in you just typing the first thing that comes to mind. Spend time thinking about what you want to include in this section and how you want it to be displayed. Whatever you do, do not overuse capital letters and do not write just one sentence. Unfortunately you are not allowed to include images, video or links in your book description, only text, but that doesn't mean it can't be presented well and help sell your product.

Include as many keywords and phrases that are related to your book as possible whilst still making it sound like a coherent and logical book description. This will help with discoverability when people are searching on Amazon for books with certain keywords.

Open a word document before you are ready to begin uploading to KDP and construct your book description.

Suggested Layout Of Your Book Description

When a potential buyer looks at a product on Amazon they will first see an image of your book, the title, and prices in different formats. This is followed by the book description. You are limited to 4000 characters but that should be more than enough to allow you to sell your product. Don't worry about putting any information in the book description about yourself, there is another section for that called Author Central which we will talk about more later.

To start with, think of a headline, this can be the tag line of your book, an amazing quote from a review, or a comparison to a more well known book. Whatever you choose, make sure it grabs the readers attention, but keep it short and punchy.

Following that needs to be the description which you can take from the back of the book if you have already written it.

"The light hearted, but charming antics of teenage detective Lawrence Pinkley will strike a chord with anyone, young or old..."

**NOT ALL EIGHTEEN YEAR OLDS WANT TO BE A DETECTIVE...
ESPECIALLY WHEN THEY DON'T HAVE A CLUE !**

THE MYSTERY OF VAN GOGH'S MISSING HEART

Teenager Lawrence Pinkley unwillingly inherits his father's Private Detective Agency on the cold north east coast of England. Despite not knowing the first thing about solving crim
a successful Private Investigator is growing.

But, when Hollywood comes to town, Pinkley stumbles into the path of the dangerously disturbed Doctor Ubel who could quickly put an end to Pinkley's short career, as well as hi:
totally impregnable. Pinkley must use all his cunning and limited intellect to find the painting whilst out foxing Doctor Ubel.

Packed with surreal and laugh-out-loud moments, The Mystery of Van Gogh's Missing Heart is a hilarious crime novel that appeals to anyone from 8 to 80 (or, come to think of it, ·

Now that you've got them interested and intrigued you need to get others to tell the reader how great the book is. Include some one-liners from reviews.

If you have written other books, list them next. A reader is more likely to buy a book from someone who has a proven track record of experience and longevity. You may have noticed when buying something from Amazon that on the product page there is often a row of book covers showing books that other people have also bought or viewed. Hopefully your other books, if you have any, will also appear here, but you cannot guarantee it, so make sure you tell them that they exist by adding them in the description.

If you still have space why not include a personal message to the reader about the book?

REVIEWS

"There is an old-school charm to this novel, with a touch of witty-humor (at times "bathroom-humor") tha illustrations are their own little masterpieces..." (Elsa Takaoka, *picturestoryebook.com*)

"Tim Flanagan's new children's book, The Curious Disappearance of Professor Brown is a great read. Even read. It has mystery, humor, and it's paced perfectly so there aren't any parts that drag.We are passenge moment be laughing, and then in the next moment will be drawn into the suspense of the story." (Maria F

Also by Tim Flanagan

Read the complete Lawrence Pinkley detective series:
The Curious Disappearance of Professor Brown
Lawrence Pinkley's Casebook. Vol. 1
Lawrence Pinkley's Casebook. Vol. 2

Tim Flanagan is also the author of the Number one Sci-Fi / Dystopian series for teens, The Moon Stealers
The Moon Stealers and the Quest for the Silver Bough (Book 1)
The Moon Stealers and the Queen of the Underworld (Book 2)
The Moon Stealers and the Everlasting Night (Book 3)
The Moon Stealers and the Children of the Light (Book 4)

A PERSONAL NOTE FROM THE AUTHOR:

When I was a child I enjoyed looking at the artwork that went with the books I read, especially those that something I wanted to recreate with The Curious Disappearance of Professor Brown. Writing can sometim Dylan Gibson, has made this book a complete joy to work on. Dylan's illustrations bring an added dimensi

Use html Formatting Tags To Change The Appearance Of The Wording

The only thing you have control over when writing your book description for the book page is whether it is in capitals or lowercase. To make it look more interesting you will need to add some simple html tags into it. It is not very complicated but will help you make bold lettering, italics, different size text as well as Amazon orange text. The letters used in the html tags count towards your character limit which is why you need to plan it carefully beforehand.

Html tags consist of an opening tag to start the specific action. It is then followed by the text you want it to apply to, then the closing tag ending the action. Copy the following tags into your book description to make it more visually inspiring. When it comes to uploading your book to KDP you will need to copy and paste your book description into the relevant space in your Book Details Page. It will look like an incoherent jumble of letters and words, but once Amazon have reviewed your book you will be able to see what it looks like on the different marketplaces. Check to make sure that it has come out the way you wanted it to before you start publicising your book - you wouldn't want anyone else to see any mistakes.

The choice of tags you can use in your Amazon description is limited and does change on occasions. You used to be able to get images into your product page but unfortunately that is no longer possible.

Amazon Approved html Tags

You will see from the following tags that there is a letter or group of letters sandwiched between < and >

It is that letter or group of letters that creates the action on the text. The tags will not show up on the final product description.

<b> ENTER TEXT TO MAKE IT BOLD </b>

<i> ENTER TEXT TO MAKE IT ITALICS </i>

<u> ENTER TEXT TO UNDERLINE IT </u>

<h1> ENTER TEXT TO MAKE IT LARGE </h2>

<h2> ENTER TEXT TO MAKE IT SLIGHTLY SMALLER BUT IN AMAZON ORANGE </h2>

<h3> ENTER TEXT TO MAKE IT SLIGHTLY SMALLER THAN H2 IN BLACK</h3>

<h4> SAME SIZE AS H3 TEXT </h4>

<h5> ENTER TEXT TO MAKE IT SLIGHTLY SMALLER THAN H3 </h5>

<h6> ENTER TEXT TO MAKE IT SLIGHTLY SMALLER THAN H5 </h6>

<hr> FOR A HORIZONTAL RULE (no closing tag needed)

 FOR A LINE BREAK (no closing tag needed)

For bullet points you need to use two tags : <ul> and <li>

<ul>
<li> ENTER TEXT FOR POINT ONE </li>
<li> ENTER TEXT FOR POINT TWO </li>
</ul>

For numbered bullet points you need to use two slightly different tags : <ol> and <li>

<ol>
<li> ENTER TEXT FOR POINT ONE </li>
<li> ENTER TEXT FOR POINT TWO </li>
</ol>

You don't have to be restricted to using one set of tags, you can use combinations of more than one at the same time if you wish. For example, you might want italic bullet points which would need the <i> tag adding into the bullet point tags. It would look something like this:

<ul>
<li> <i> ENTER TEXT FOR POINT ONE </i> </li>
<li> <i> ENTER TEXT FOR POINT TWO </i> </li>
</ul>

html Tag Example:

The following code was put into an Amazon KDP description so that you can see what it looks like when it has been published onto an Amazon website. You can download a pdf copy by going to www.smarturl.it/APMHTMLTable

HTML DESCRIPTION TAGS

<b> Example of BOLD text </b>
<i> Example of ITALIC text </i>
<u> Example of UNDERLINED text </u>

<h1> Example of H1 text </h1>

<h2> Example of H2 text </h2>

<h3> Example of H3 text </h3>

<h4> Example of H4 text </h4>

<h5> Example of H5 text </h5>

<h6> Example of H6 text </h6>

<hr>

That's a HORIZONTAL RULE above, and this…

…is a LINE BREAK
Example of bullet points:
<ul>
<li> Bullet point one </li>
<li> Bullet point two </li>
</ul>

Example of numbered bullet points:
<ol>
<li> Numbered point one </li>
<li> Numbered point two </li>
</ol>

Combining tags - bullet points with italic text:
<ul>
<li> <i> Bullet point one </i> </li>
<li> <i> Bullet point one </i> </li>
</ul>

Example of BOLD text
Example of ITALIC text
Example of UNDERLINED text

Example of H1 text

Example of H2 text

Example of H3 text

Example of H4 text

Example of H5 text

Example of H6 text

That's a HORIZONTAL RULE above, and this…

…is a LINE BREAK
Example of bullet points:

- Bullet point one
- Bullet point two

Example of numbered bullet points:

1. Numbered point one
2. Numbered point two

Combining tags - bullet points with italic text:

- *Bullet point one*
- *Bullet point one*

11. ISBN Numbers

ISBN stands for an International Standard Book Number and is assigned to every book that is published. However, eBooks published through KDP do not have to have one and can be published without. ISBN numbers apply to only one version of a book and cannot be used for other versions even if the book is the same but in a different format. For example, the ISBN for a print version of your book cannot be used for the eBook version. The product pages for eBooks do not show the ISBN, only the ASIN which is a code automatically assigned to your book by Amazon.

From January 1, 2015, Italy changed their VAT law on eBooks. If it has an ISBN they only charge 4% VAT on a book purchased in their country. If it doesn't have an ISBN they will charge 22% VAT. This only applies to eBooks sold in Italy. No other country has so far followed suit.

If you decide to buy an ISBN for your eBook the official place to go is www.isbn.org. Prices start from $125 for one ISBN but with bigger discounts for volume purchases.

If you have your own ISBN, input it into the relevant box in section one of the KDP Book Publishing Pages. If you haven't got one, leave the box empty.

ISBN (optional) (What's this?)

12. Choosing Categories

When you look on an Amazon sales page you will see that every book is listed under different categories. The problem is that the categories you see in an Amazon store are not necessarily the same as the ones you can choose from when you are inputting the information into your Book Details Page. Only the main categories can be selected when you complete your KDP Book Details Page, and you're limited to two. The smaller sub categories can be selected by including certain words in your title, subtitle, description and keywords.

To choose the categories you wish to place your book in, you will first need to go to your local Amazon store and open the Kindle Bestseller list. There is a list of main categories on the left side that opens into sub categories when you click on them.

‹ Any Department
‹ Kindle Store
  Kindle eBooks
    Arts & Photography
    Biographies & Memoirs
    Business & Money
    Children's eBooks
    Comics & Graphic Novels
    Computers & Technology
    Cookbooks, Food & Wine
    Crafts, Hobbies & Home
    Education & Teaching
    Foreign Languages
    Health, Fitness & Dieting
    History
    Humor & Entertainment
    Lesbian, Gay, Bisexual & Transgender eBooks
    Literature & Fiction
    Mystery, Thriller & Suspense
    Nonfiction
    Parenting & Relationships
    Politics & Social Sciences
    Professional & Technical
    Reference
    Religion & Spirituality
    Romance
    Science & Math
    Science Fiction & Fantasy
    Self-Help
    Sports & Outdoors
    Teen & Young Adult
    Travel

Working from the Amazon marketplace page, choose a main category that you think your book would fall into and write it down on a piece of paper. Click the main category and you will see another layer of categories has opened up. Click a sub category that could be relevant to your book (no matter how vague the connection). That might open up another layer of options. Keep working through until no further sub categories open up. Write down the pathway you used to get there.

For example: If I wrote a teen fantasy book about altered world events, my category pathway would be:

Kindle eBooks > Science Fiction & Fantasy > Fantasy > Alternative History

Go back and make alterations to create additional pathways. By doing this you can see the words and phrases that are available and consistently relevant to your book.

Before you continue, go to Appendix A, B and C at the back of this book to see the complete category options that you have available to you.

Now you need to compare the pathways you discovered in the Amazon store with the options you have available on KDP. And this is where it becomes vague, because the options you have on KDP don't match those in the Amazon marketplace.

In the example I gave above, there is no Science Fiction & Fantasy option to select in KDP. There are two separate options, one for science Fiction and a separate one for Fantasy. If I select Fantasy there isn't the Alternative History sub category option that there was at the Amazon store. But, there is a category of its own called Alternative History, so I might consider putting it in there. There is also a separate list for juvenile fiction which includes an option called Fantasy & Magic, but nothing more specific, so I might consider putting it in there too.

There are many books that tell you how to analyse categories to choose the best place to put your book, but if that analysis is based on the category listings on the Amazon marketplace, you cannot then translate that to your KDP Book Details Page. To start with, select two options you think specifically match your book whilst avoiding huge general categories, then use keywords to narrow your category selection and make it more relevant. Try to pick two categories that are different to each other. You can always try putting your book in alternative categories at a later stage.

13. Sub Category Keywords

Although you get to choose two categories for your book to be listed in, the sub categories that you see in the Amazon marketplace often do not appear as options to choose from when publishing your book. The sub category listings can be achieved by using specific keywords. Amazon catalogues your book into various sub categories by the appearance of very specific keywords relating to your book. As you are only allowed to choose seven keywords for each book, only use a maximum of two keywords from the genre specific lists below to increase your chance of appearing in a relevant sub category.

Before you go any further, go to Appendix D and E at the back of this book to see the sub category options that might be relevant to your book.

These sub category keywords aren't necessarily restricted to the keyword section of your KDP Book Details Page. You can also work them into the subtitle of your book and description. Adding them to the title of your book can look messy and often doesn't make much sense, but most books don't have a subtitle, so adding them there can often work. All you need to do is make the keywords sound relevant to the book.

A note about Textbooks: If you have used Amazon's Textbook Creator you might want to include the keyword phrase:

kdp_textbook_submission

This keyword phrase (together with underscores) needs to be included in the Keyword options in section three Target Your Book to Customers in the KDP Book Details Page for your Textbook to be included in the Textbook Category.

Choosing your sub category keywords

Scan through the lists to find one or two sub categories that you would like your book to appear in and check to see what the keyword or phrase is that you need to use.

For example, if you've written a Historical Crime book for children that is set in the 19th century, you might include the following keywords:

19th century, detective

These are two keywords that you could use in your seven keyword allocation, but you could also use them in your subtitle : 19th Century Detective Book for Children.

It sounds relevant to the book, but includes the two keywords to help get it seen in the relevant sub categories.

At the moment these category keywords only seem to apply to amazon.com and don't necessarily work with other marketplaces.

14. Keywords

When readers are buying from Amazon they search the website in one of two ways - they either browse through categories and look at the top 100 in a particular genre or theme, or they go to the search bar and enter the specific name of a book they have heard of, or a general phrase. Keywords are the words or phrases that readers put into the Amazon search bar to find what they are looking for. Your book will need seven carefully chosen keywords or phrases to help people discover it.

Theoretically you should use keywords that only relate to your book, but how will that help readers find a book they don't know about? So, you need to think around the themes, concepts and genres of your book.

We have already mentioned using keywords to get listed in sub categories, but now we need to find some words that are more specifically relevant to the content of your book. We need to come up with more keywords or phrases.

The easiest way to decide on keywords is to search through Amazon yourself to see which words turn up.

How To Use Amazon's Search Engine

Start by getting a piece of paper and writing down some words or phrases that are relevant to your book.

For example, if I'm writing a book about aliens I might try using words like: alien, aliens, ufos, martians, science fiction, etc

Write down as many as you can think of. Even adding a letter like the additional "s" onto "aliens" can bring up all sorts of alternative possibilities. When you have a comprehensive list, open up amazon.com, go to the search bar and select "Kindle Store" so that you're only searching through other Kindle books.

Using the example from above, let's start by typing "alien" into the search bar.

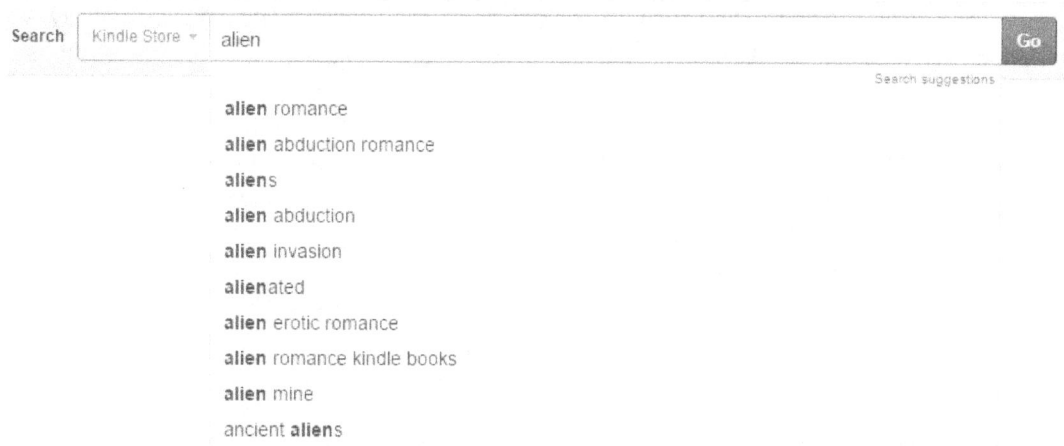

You can see that Amazon's search engine throws up ten of the most popular search terms beginning with "alien". These are ten more search terms that you could possible use, but it would be a better use of your time to concentrate on a maximum of five terms from this list that are the most relevant to your book and appear highest on the list. The higher they are the more they are searched for.

Let's say that the book I'm trying to create keywords for does not include anything romantic. That would discount some of the terms immediately and leave me with aliens, alien abduction, alien invasion, alienated, alien mine and ancient aliens. I am going to take the first three from that list and add them to my piece of paper. Do this for all your other search words and expand your list. It doesn't matter if there are loads of words or phrases on the list, you are going to narrow them down even more.

When you have created your list, go back to the Amazon search bar and start with the first word or phrase and see what results are provided. In this example I type "alien" once again and press return to see the first page of books that are linked to the word "alien".

1-16 of 17,022 results for **Kindle Store** : "alien"

As you can see, the word "alien" is a pretty big and well populated search term with over seventeen thousand results. If you included the word alien as one of your keywords, you would probably get lost amongst all the other books and never noticed. So beside the word "alien" on your bit of paper, write down the total number of results.

Before we move on, take a look at the first five books on that page. The books are not ordered by publication date, nor by the number of reviews or price or bestseller ranking. What makes them appear high on the list is how relevant they are (the default setting on Amazon search results). Relevance is achieved by including the word alien in your title, subtitle, description, and keywords. This is why you also need to think carefully about adding a subtitle with sub category specific keywords included in it, as well as including them in the description.

Do the same for the other terms:

1-16 of 17,025 results for **Kindle Store** : "aliens"

1-16 of 1,062 results for **Kindle Store** : "alien abduction"

1-16 of 1,907 results for **Kindle Store** : "alien invasion"

You can see that there is a big difference between the two terms "alien" and "aliens", and the other two terms "alien abduction" and "alien invasion". If we go through the five words we started with - alien, aliens, ufos, martians, and science fiction - we would have a list that looked something like this:

KEYWORD RESULTS

Keyword / Phrase	Total Results
Alien	17,022
Aliens	17,025
Alien abduction	1,062
Alien invasion	1,907
Aliens and ufos	1,979
Ufos	4,272
Ufos and aliens	1,981
ufos fiction	1,561
Martians	546
science fiction	129,754
Science fiction and fantasy	48,857
Science fiction best sellers	455

This shows the number of results for each keyword or phrase that is relevant to the book I am preparing. It would be wise to instantly dismiss large search results like Science Fiction, and Science Fiction and Fantasy. Although they will be popular search terms your book will struggle to reach the front of the queue. Alien and aliens can also go. I would take Science Fiction best sellers as that is likely to be a popular search term and doesn't have too many books featured in the list. The word Martian doesn't have many results either so might make a good keyword, but Alien abduction will probably prove more popular even though it has more results.

If I take these two phrases and add them to the two words I have already chosen for my sub categories I still need to think of three more.

For the following three you need to look at which books are similar to your book and are popular at the moment.

Go back to Amazon and go to the Kindle eBook store and open up the Bestsellers chart.

On the left side of the screen you will see the categories listed. Find a main category that is relevant to your book. For our example, our alien book is for adults so I will open the Science Fiction & Fantasy category.

‹ Any Department

‹ Kindle Store

‹ Kindle eBooks

Science Fiction &
Fantasy

Fantasy

Science Fiction

Don't go into any of the sub categories. You will now see the current top 100 books listed in Science Fiction & Fantasy. Open up a separate second window that is also open at the Kindle store, you are going to use this window to search the results you see in the top 100 Science Fiction & Fantasy books.

Type the title of the first book in the Bestseller list into the search bar in the second window and press return. You will see all the results for that title. Each page lists 16 results. You need to find a title that has sixteen or less results so that your book appears in the first page. If the first book in the Bestseller list has 17 or more results move on to the second book and so on.

Keep going until your have found three more keywords or phrases. These keywords will need to be changed on a regular basis to keep up with changes in the Bestseller listings. Don't even bother checking book titles that are massively popular such as Harry Potter, Hunger Games etc or even very popular author names - they will almost always be rejected by Amazon.

You now have seven keywords or phrases that consist of:

2 Sub category keywords
2 Researched relevant keywords
3 Relevant bestseller keywords

This is a good mix of different keywords, but they will need changing on a regular basis.

15. Pre-Orders

So that you can start promoting and marketing your new book as soon as possible, KDP now have the facility to allow readers to pre-order your book up to 90 days before it is due to be released.

When you complete the KDP Book Details Page you will see in section four that it asks you to select when your book will be released. Click the button beside "Make my book available for pre-order" and you will be given a calendar box to select your release date.

4. Select Your Book Release Option

Please select if you are ready to release your book immediately or if you would like to make it available for pre-order (What's this?)

○ I am ready to release my book now
● Make my book available for pre-order

Set a release date for your book

[   ]

Once you have completed all the other sections and pressed publish, your book will be available for pre-order in Amazon stores as soon as it has been approved. Readers will see the normal book sales page together with a pre-order label giving the date when it will become available.

Hungry In Texas (The Hunger Series Book 1) May 15, 2015 | Kindle eBook
by Lisa Blackstone

$2.99 Kindle Edition

Pre-order with 1-Click ®

Available for Pre-order. This item will be released on May 15, 2015.

Although a reader will be able to order the book it won't actually be delivered to them until the official release date. Each sale you get during this pre order period effects your sales ranking pushing the book further up the category listings for even more people to discover, as if it was available in the normal way. The sales page will function as normal, except that customers will not be able to download a sample of the book. After the release date samples will be available as per normal. Customers are not charged for the download until the book becomes available, therefore you will also not receive your royalty until the book becomes available.

Release dates start from just after midnight eastern time on your chosen day. Pre-order books can be available on all Amazon marketplaces except in India. To be eligible for a Pre-order, your book must be a new book and not a public domain work. Only ten books can be listed at one time for pre-orders.

To make the pre-order book available you will need to upload a version of the book, whether a draft manuscript of the book or the final version, in section six of the KDP Book Details Page.

To enable pre-order for your book, at this time you must submit either the final version of your book file or a draft manuscript. (Why?)

○ This is the final version of my book for release.
● This is a draft manuscript and is not ready for release.

Even if your book is not yet ready, you can still upload the manuscript as it is. This is not the version that will get published but to make it available for pre-order Amazon will need something. When you have the final manuscript ready you will need to go back into your KDP Bookshelf, select the book and upload the final book file then click save. This has to be done no later than midnight eastern time ten days before the release date otherwise Amazon will ban you from using the pre-order facility for one year.

You will receive a report listing all of the orders placed and cancelled during the pre-order period.

16. Amazon Royalties

Getting Paid

Whichever country your books sell in, they will accumulate royalties. If you have selected to receive your royalties by Electronic Fund Transfer (EFT) your royalties will be paid into your nominated back account in your local currency sixty days after the end of the month the balance was accrued. If you are being paid by check, your payment will be made sixty days after the end of the month that the minimum threshold was reached.

Choosing A Royalty Percentage

KDP allows you to choose between two different royalty percentages - 35% and 70%. Your instinctive choice would be to go for the 70% option so that you earn more money, but both of them have different benefits.

When choosing your royalty option, consider the following:

- **The Price Of The Book.** The price you want to list your book at will effect which royalty option you can use. Books priced between $0.99 and $200 can use the 35% royalty option, whereas books priced $2.99 to $9.99 can use the 70% royalty plan.

- **Delivery Costs.** 35% royalty plans do not get charged delivery costs. 70% royalty plans get charged a delivery cost according to the number of megabytes your book contains.

DELIVERY COSTS

Marketplace	Delivery Cost per MB
Amazon.com	US $0.15/MB
Amazon.com.in	INR ₹7/MB
Amazon.ca	CAD $0.15/MB
Amazon.com.br	BRL R$0.30/MB
Amazon.co.uk	UK £0.10/MB
Amazon.de	€0,12/MB
Amazon.fr	€0,12/MB
Amazon.es	€0,12/MB
Amazon.it	€0,12/MB
Amazon.nl	€0,12/MB
Amazon.co.jp	¥1/MB
Amazon.com.mx	MXN $1/MB
Amazon.com.au	AUD $0.15/MB

- **Available Territories.** Choosing the 35% royalty option allows your book to be available in any territory. 70% royalty options will only be paid on books bought in the following countries - Andorra, Australia (including territories Christmas Island (CX), Cocos Keeling Islands (CC),Heard & McDonald Islands (HM), and Northfolk Island (NF)), Austria, Belgium, Canada, France, Great Britain, Guernsey, Germany, Gibraltar, Italy, Ireland, Isle of Man, Jersey, Lichtenstein, Luxembourg, Monaco, Netherlands, New Zealand (including territories Cook Islands (CK), Niue (NU), and Tokelau), San Marino, Switzerland, Spain, United Kingdom, United States, Vatican City. Any sales in a country outside of these territories will be paid at the 35% rate.

- **KDP Select**. If you enrol on KDP Select you will also be able to receive 70% royalties in Brazil, Japan, Mexico and India, otherwise it is 35%.

If you choose the 70% royalty option, you must ensure that the price you choose is 20% cheaper on Amazon than the list price for the same book in printed or digital forms on other sales channels, including your own website.

Books that contain primarily public domain content cannot use the 70% royalty option.

Books in the 70% royalty option will still receive 70% of sales when you participate in Matchbook or Countdown Deals, even if the price drops below the minimum list price that would normally be required if your to keep your book in the 70% list price bracket.

Books in the 35% royalty option have the option to be removed from the Kindle Book Lending scheme. 70% royalty option books must remain in the scheme.

How Are Royalties Calculated

Royalties are calculated according to the list price in the different territories. If you are running a promotion you will earn royalties based on the promotional list price, not the original list price.

For 35% royalty rate:
35% x Amazon list price

For 70% royalty rate:
70% x (Amazon list price - delivery costs)

VAT On List Prices

You will notice that your list price in the UK and European Amazon stores will also include VAT which varies between countries. Your royalty will be based on the list price before local VAT is added.

From January 1, 2015, Italy changed their tax law on eBooks according to whether a book has an ISBN number or not. Ebooks sold without an ISBN will be charged 22% VAT, whilst those with an ISBN will be charged 4%.

17. Kindle Matchbook

When you are completing your KDP Book Details Page you will notice that there is a button you can select that allows you to enrol in the Kindle MatchBook program.

10. Kindle MatchBook

☐ Enroll this book in the Kindle MatchBook program. (Details)

When you enrol in the MatchBook program it enables customers who have already bought the printed version of the same book via Amazon, to purchase the Kindle version for $2.99, $1.99, $0.99 or even free. The idea is to offer them a Kindle book at a discounted rate. If you don't have a printed version of your book available, then you do not need to enrol in MatchBook, but if you do it might be worth enrolling just on the chance of up selling to someone who has already bought your book. It provides the customer with the opportunity to read your book in different formats on different platforms wherever they are.

You will still receive a royalty payment for that Kindle sale, but at the discounted price that you select. Your royalty percentage will be based on the original list price. For example, if the original list price was $3.99 and you were receiving 70% royalties, a MatchBook price at $1.99 will generate 70% royalties even though it has gone below the $2.99 threshold that would normally mean you would only be eligible for the 35% royalty.

If a reader has purchased your printed book from somewhere other than Amazon, the MatchBook promotional offer will not be available to them. All books are eligible for MatchBook, but there has to be a printed version that is also sold by Amazon. The promotional price must be 50% or less than the regular list price. You can enrol existing titles as well as new titles on MatchBook and you do not need to be enrolled on KDP Select to be able to participate. You can remove yourself from the MatchBook scheme whenever you wish by un-checking the box in section ten of the KDP Details Page and resubmitting your book to Amazon.

18. Kindle Book Lending

Kindle Book Lending is a feature that can be found in section eleven of the KDP Book Details Page. The scheme allows readers the option to lend books on Amazon to their friends and family for a duration of 14 days. The original reader can only lend the book to one person and cannot read it themselves whilst it is on loan.

11. Kindle Book Lending

✓ Allow lending for this book (Details)

You will probably notice that when you get to section eleven of the KDP Book Details Page that the option is already selected for you. Amazon automatically enrol you in this scheme and only titles in the 35% royalty option have the opportunity to opt out. 70% royalty titles cannot change this setting and must participate.

You will not receive a royalty payment on the loan of the book, only the original purchase. Unfortunately there is no way of knowing how often your books are being loaned. If you opt out of the Kindle Book Lending scheme, customers who purchased the book before you opted out will still be able to lend the book if they wish.

19. Publishing Your Book

Now that you have written your book, had it edited and formatted, got an eye catching cover, used html tags in your description, and carefully planned your keywords and categories, you can now begin uploading it to Amazon so that it is ready for publication.

Log in to your KDP dashboard, click "Bookshelf" then "Add new title".

Add new title

The first thing you need to do is decide if you want your book to be enrolled in the KDP Select program or not. If you do, click the check box next to "Enroll this book in KDP Select".

Introducing KDP Select

Take advantage of KDP Select, an optional program that makes your book exclusive to Kindle and eligible for the following benefits:

- **Reach more readers** - With each 90-day enrollment period, your book will appear in Kindle Unlimited in the U.S., U.K., Italy, Spain, Germany, France and Brazil and the Kindle Owners' Lending Library (KOLL) in the U.S, U.K., Germany, France, and Japan which can help readers discover your book.
- **Earn more money** - Every time your book is selected and read past 10% from Kindle Unlimited or borrowed from KOLL, you'll earn your share of the monthly KDP Select Global Fund. You can also earn a 70% royalty for sales to customers in Japan, Brazil, India and Mexico.
- **Maximize your sales potential** - Choose from two promotional tools including: Kindle Countdown Deals, time-bound promotional discounts for your book, available on Amazon.com and Amazon.co.uk, while earning royalties; or Free Book Promotion, where readers can get your book free for a limited time.

Learn more

☐ **Enroll this book in KDP Select**

By checking this box, you are enrolling in KDP Select for 90 days. Books enrolled in KDP Select must not be available in digital format on any other platform during their enrollment. If your book is found to be available elsewhere in digital format, it may not be eligible to remain in the program. See the KDP Select Terms and Conditions and KDP Select FAQs for more information.

1. Enter Your Book Details

Input your book title and subtitle if you have one. Subtitles are limited to 200 characters. Both the book title and subtitle should not contain any other words such as best selling, free, other promotional terms, other authors names or books. Amazon may reject or unpublish your book if you use unnecessary words.

1. Enter Your Book Details

Book name

New Title 1

Please enter the exact title only. Books submitted with extra words in this field will not be published. (Why?)

Subtitle (optional)

Please enter the exact subtitle only. Books submitted with extra words in this field will not be published. (Why?)

If this book is one in a series, click the box and input the name of the series together with which volume number it is. Only input a number (1,2,3 etc) rather than words. Amazon will automatically link all books in a series and put them on a separate landing page. On your book sales page, Amazon will list the series name and display which number the book is in that series, together with a link to the series landing page.

☑ This book is part of a series (What's this?)

Series title   Volume

Which edition is this version of your book. If this is the first time it has been published enter the number 1, if it has been published before and you are uploading a new version, input the relevant number.

Who is the publisher? If it is yourself, you can leave this field empty. If are signed to a publishing company, you can enter their name here or use the name of your own publishing label.

You now need to cut and paste the winning description you've already prepared into the "Description" box.

Description (What's this?)

4000 characters left

Book contributors: (What's this?)

Add contributors

Language (What's this?)

English

ISBN (optional) (What's this?)

Click the "Add Contributors" button to start adding the people who are responsible for your book. The first person should be you. Enter your first name and last name then what your role was in creating the book from the drop down menu. If you wish to add another contributor click the "Add another" button and fill in the same fields for that person. Do not feel that you have to add every single person that was involved with the book. Usually it is sufficient to just put yourself in as the author. Include any other authors that are involved with the book, as well as illustrators. Anyone else can be included in an acknowledgements page inside the book.

Add or Change contributors   ×

First (or Given) name: Last name (or Surname):   Title:

[   ]   [   ]   [Select title   ⇕]   [Remove]

[Add another]

                                                                    [Save]   [Cancel]

Once you have finished, click "Save" and return to your Book Details Page.

Next, select the language the book was written in and add an ISBN number if you have one.

2. Verify Your Publishing Rights

You need to ensure that you hold the publishing rights to your book.

2. Verify Your Publishing Rights

Verify Your Publishing Rights (What's this?)

○ This is a public domain work.

○ This is not a public domain work and I hold the necessary publishing rights.

If you have written the book and it contains no text or images that are not your own, then you own all the publishing rights to the book and you need to check the "This is not a public domain work and I hold the necessary publishing rights" button. If your book contains information that is someone else's you need to check to see if the copyright notice has expired and is in the public domain. Duration of copyright varies between countries so you might not be able to publish your book in every country. If your book contains public domain work, check the button next to "This is a public domain work".

3. Target Your Book To Customers

During the preparation for publication we chose two categories for your book to appear in. This is the section where you need to enter them.

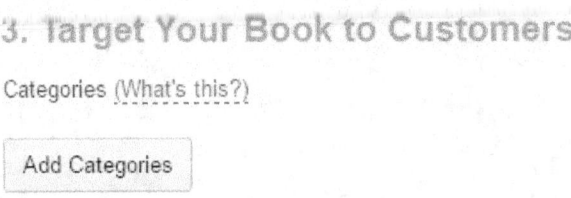

Click "Add Categories" to open another window where you will be able to select the two categories. The categories that are available for you to use are not always the same as those that appear in the Amazon bestseller listings which is why you need to do some research on this before publishing. Once you've selected two categories click "Save".

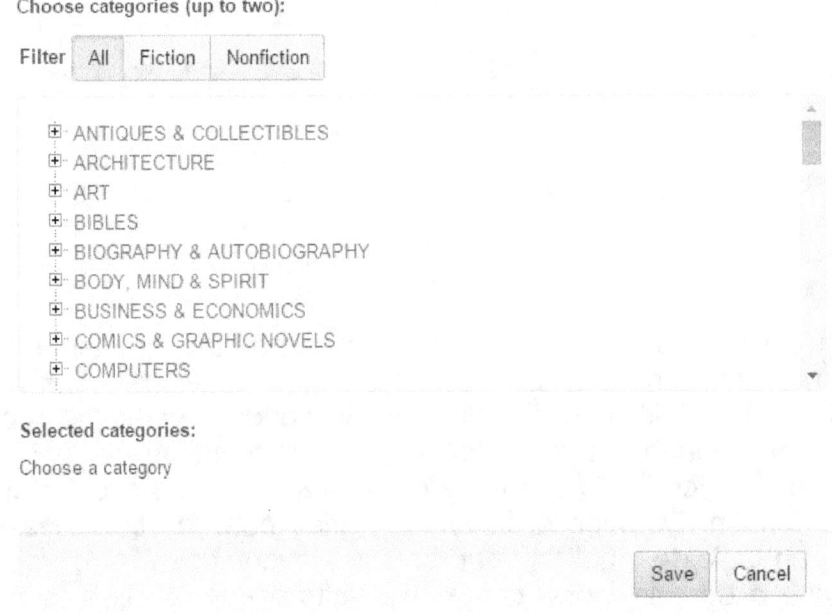

Next, choose the age range that your book is targeted at.

Age Range (optional) (What's this?)

Minimum

| Select ⬍ |

Maximum

| Select ⬍ |

U.S. Grade Range (optional) (What's this?)

Minimum

| Select ⬍ |

Maximum

| Select ⬍ |

These are optional fields but including them helps a reader to find books that are suitable. It also helps books to be categorized correctly, particularly if you are publishing a book aimed at a younger audience.

Here is a general guide to ages and grades, as well as suitable books.

AGE RANGE GUIDE

Age Range	US Grade Levels	Book Type
0 - 2	Baby	Picture board books
3 - 5	Pre School	Picture books
6 - 8	Kindergarten - 2nd Grade	Early readers
9 - 12	3rd - 6th Grade	Middle Grade chapter books
13 - 18	7th - 12th Grade	Teen & Young adult chapter books

You now need to input the seven keywords or phrases you have prepared for your book, each one separated by a comma.

Search keywords (up to 7, optional) (What's this?)

| |

7 keywords left

4. Select Your Book Release Option

4. Select Your Book Release Option

Please select if you are ready to release your book immediately or if you would like to make it available for pre-order (What's this?)

○ I am ready to release my book now
○ Make my book available for pre-order

Here you can select if your book is ready for immediate release or whether you are making your book available for pre-order. If your book is ready, check the "I am ready to release my book now" button, or alternatively the "Make my book available for pre-order" and chose a date for release that is up to 90 days ahead.

5. Upload Or Create A Book Cover

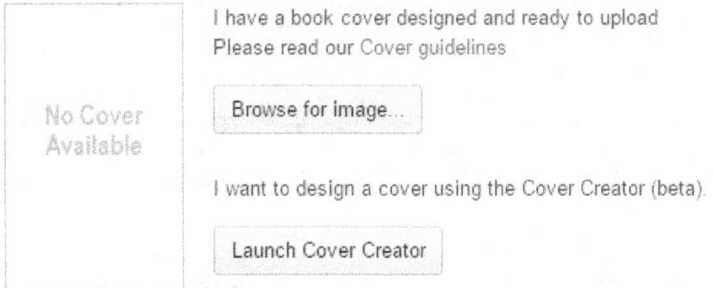

If you have already got a cover, click on the "Browse for Image" button to find it on your computer. Once the image has been successfully uploaded you will see it appear in the box on the left and you should see the following message:

Or, alternatively, click the "Launch Cover Creator" to create your cover.

6. Upload Your Book File

6. Upload Your Book File

Select a digital rights management (DRM) option: (What's this?)

○ Enable digital rights management
◉ Do not enable digital rights management

Before you upload your book file, you need to decide whether you want to enable Digital Rights Management or not. This protects your books from being shared. If you want to protect your books, click "Enable Digital Rights Management", however, if you are happy for readers to share your work, click on "Do Not Enable Digital Rights Management".

If you have made your book available for pre-order, you will also see the following option:

To enable pre-order for your book, at this time you must submit either the final version of your book file or a draft manuscript. (Why?)

○ This is the final version of my book for release.
◉ This is a draft manuscript and is not ready for release.

Select what stage your book is at.

Once this is done you need to upload your book or draft manuscript. Click the "Browse" button and find the file on your computer and click upload.

Book content file:

Browse

It may take some time depending on how much memory your book takes up so be patient. Once you have successfully uploaded your book you should receive two messages.

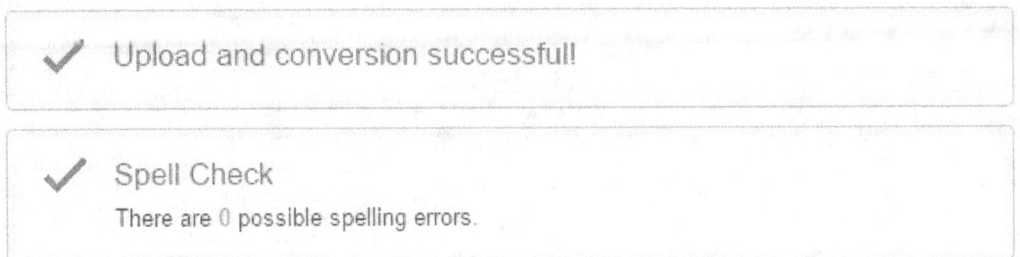

The first confirms that your upload was successful, the second tells you the results of an automatic spell check. If you have some spelling errors open the window and have a look at them. Amazon flags up any word that it doesn't recognize so made up names and unusual words will all have been identified as mistakes. If any are ones that slipped through the net, go back to your original manuscript on your computer, make the necessary changes then re-upload. If none of the spelling errors need changing, click on "Ignore" and move on to the next section.

7. Preview Your Book

Once your book has been uploaded it is a good idea to preview it so that you can see what it might look like on the end user's eReader.

7. Preview Your Book

Previewing your book is an integral part of the publishing process and the best way to guarantee that your readers will have a good experience and see the book you want them to see. KDP offers two options to preview your book depending on your needs. Which should I use?

Online Previewer

For most users, the online previewer is the best and easiest way to preview your content. The online previewer allows you to preview most books as they will appear on Kindle, Kindle Fire, iPad, and iPhone. If your book is fixed layout (for more information on fixed layout, see the Kindle Publishing Guidelines), the online previewer will display your book as it will appear on Kindle Fire.

Preview book

When you click " Preview book" you will be taken to a new window with a simulation of your book on a Kindle device.

As with the end user, the reader can choose what size font they want to read your book in. Increasing or decreasing the font size will change the layout of the book and any pictures you may have included inside it. You can also change the device you are using to see how your book would look on different size screens, including Kindle Fire HDX, HDX 8.9, Fire Phone, Kindle Voyage, Kindle DX, iPhone, iPad, Android Phone, and Android Tablet. Once you are happy with it, click the "Book Details" link in the top left corner to return back to the Book Details Page.

Click on "Save and Continue" to go through to the second page to determine your pricing structure.

8. Verify Your Publishing Territories

If you have the rights to distribute your book all over the world, check the option "Worldwide rights - all territories", otherwise choose the individual territories from the list of countries.

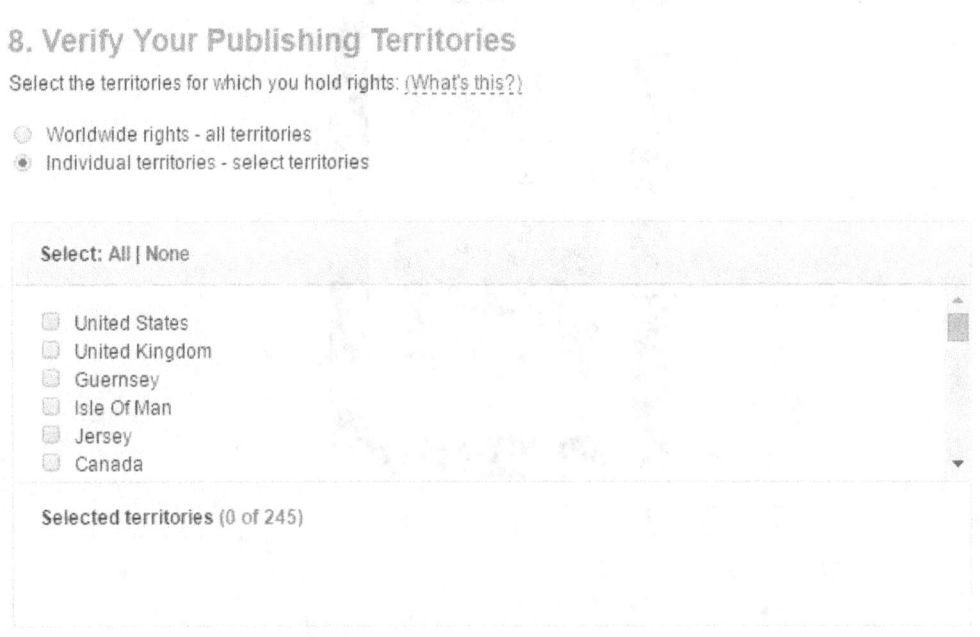

9. Set Your Pricing And Royalty

In this section you will need to decide the price of your book in different countries as well as what percentage royalty you wish to receive. Amazon have created a handy service to help you with this called KDP Pricing Support.

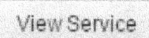

9. Set Your Pricing and Royalty

KDP Pricing Support (Beta)

See the relationship between price and past sales and author earnings for KDP books like yours.

View Service

Click "View Service" to open a new window. Amazon will analyse all of the data from your book and match it to similar books to suggest a price point that will generate the highest amount of earnings.

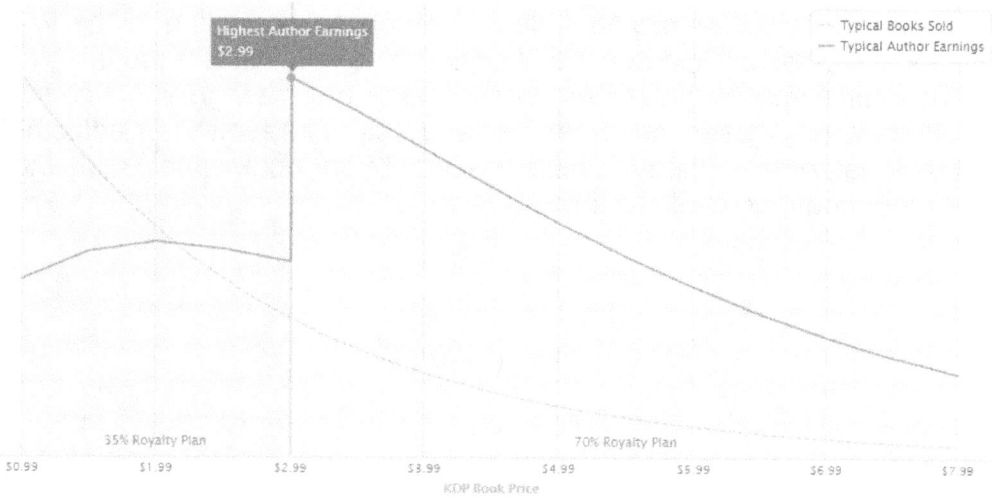

Although the number of sales decline as the price increases, because the $2.99 point is when you jump from 35% to 70% royalties this is often the best price to set your books at. You do not have to accept the advice of this service, but if you do, click the "Yes" option at the bottom of the screen and you will return to your Book Details Page with the pricing automatically completed for you. If you do not want to use this price, click "No, back to Rights and Pricing".

If you decide to set the price yourself you will first need to choose from the two royalty options - 35% or 70%. Refer back to the section comparing the benefits of the two different royalty levels, then type in the price you wish to sell your book for on amazon.com and you will see a breakdown of delivery costs, as well as royalties.

	List Price		Royalty Rate	Delivery Costs	Estimated Royalty
Amazon.com	$ 2.99	USD	35% (Why?)	n/a	$1.05
	Price must be between $2.99 and $9.99.		70%	$0.08	$2.04

You will also notice that the other territories you have selected for distribution have also been automatically completed according to the value of their local currency, based on the US price. You can still change this if you wish. To alter some of the prices, uncheck the box next to "Set [country] price automatically based on US price" and you will receive an adjustable price box together with price restrictions so that your book is not wildly more expensive or cheaper in different countries.

	Set UK price automatically based on US price				
Amazon.co.uk	£ 2.55	GBP	70%	£0.05	£1.75
	Price must be between £1.49 and £7.81.				

Once you have completed all of the different territories for your pricing, scroll down to the next section.

10. Kindle Matchbook

10. Kindle MatchBook

☐ Enroll this book in the Kindle MatchBook program. (Details)

If you have decided to participate in the Kindle MatchBook program check this box and select a price from the drop down menu. MatchBook allows people who have purchased the print version of your book from Amazon to also purchase the Kindle version of the same book at a cheaper price, or even for free. If you don't have a print version of your book you do not need to check this box.

11. Kindle Book Lending

11. Kindle Book Lending

☑ Allow lending for this book (Details)

All books are automatically enrolled in the Kindle Book Lending scheme where readers can lend your book to their friends and family for up to 14 days. If your book is in the 35% royalty option you may opt out of the Book Lending scheme.

The only thing left to do is to click the box confirming you have the necessary rights to the book and you are being compliant to KDP's Terms and Conditions and click "Save and Publish".

☐ By clicking Save and Publish below, I confirm that I have all rights necessary to make the content I am uploading available for marketing, distribution and sale in each territory I have indicated above, and that I am in compliance with the KDP Terms and Conditions.

<< Back to Your Bookshelf   Save and Publish   Save as Draft

You will then receive one final message confirming that your book is being reviewed and will take up to 12 hours for English language books, and up to 48 hours for other language books to be approved and made available for purchase on Amazon.

Publishing...

Please be aware that it can take up to 12 hours for English and 48 hours for other languages to be available for purchase in the Amazon Kindle Store. Until then, the book's status will be "In Review" on your Bookshelf.

Back to Your Bookshelf

PART TWO: ONLINE TOOLS

20. Ranking

Soon after your book has been published and you have had your first sale or two, you will begin to see a ranking number for your book appear on the sales page.

Amazon Bestsellers Rank: #71,019 Paid in Kindle Store (See Top 100 Paid in Kindle Store)
    #9 in Kindle Store > Books > Children's eBooks > Mysteries & Detectives > **Detectives**
    #77 in Kindle Store > Books > Children's eBooks > Literature & Fiction > Humourous

This ranking is specific to that particular book, not you as the author. You will see from the example above that the first number is where the book has ranked in the entire Kindle Store - this is known as the Bestseller Rank. The following two rankings relate to the books ranking within two different categories and sub categories - these are known as the Category Ranks.

Lower numbered ranks are better than higher ones - you want to aim for number one. The lower the number the more popular your book is in the store and category at that particular moment in time.

Bestseller Ranks will begin to appear once a book has sold at least one copy, although Category Ranks only begin to show when your book features in the top 100 of that particular category or sub category.

Rankings are updated hourly. The more books you sell the higher you will rank, however, recent sales will effect your ranking in a greater way than older sales. For example if you sold 50 books in one day you will shoot up the rankings a lot quicker than if you sold 25 books last week and another 25 books this week, even though the number of books sold is the same.

Do not use your sales as the only gauge to determine how successful or not a marketing campaign has been as there are many variables that cause your book to fluctuate in the Bestseller Ranks, including the performance of everyone else's books. This is also why a single sale may have a dramatic effect on the ranking if other authors' books aren't selling much, or conversely, a single sale might have very little effect on ranking if other authors are selling more books than you. Rankings are also based on the books sales history and how consistent it sells.

There is a separate Bestsellers list for free books. If you have a free promotional deal on your book through KDP Select you will see your rankings change from the paid lists into the free lists. How successful your free promotion is will also influence your ranking when the promotion ends and your book reverts back to the paid list.

Downloads through the Kindle Unlimited and Lending Library all count towards the ranking, and appear to carry the same weighting as a fully paid sale.

21. Reports

Once you have published your book you will want to know when and where it has sold. This data can give you clues as to how successful or not some of your promotions and campaigns have been.

Log in to your KDP account and click "Reports".

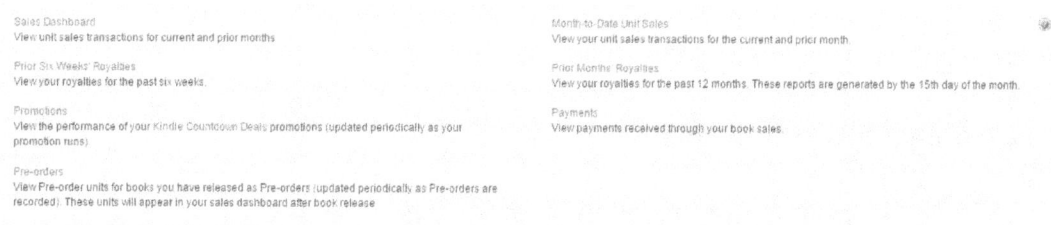

Sales Dashboard
View unit sales transactions for current and prior months

Prior Six Weeks' Royalties
View your royalties for the past six weeks.

Promotions
View the performance of your Kindle Countdown Deals promotions (updated periodically as your promotion runs).

Pre-orders
View Pre-order units for books you have released as Pre-orders (updated periodically as Pre-orders are recorded). These units will appear in your sales dashboard after book release

Month-to-Date Unit Sales
View your unit sales transactions for the current and prior month.

Prior Months' Royalties
View your royalties for the past 12 months. These reports are generated by the 15th day of the month.

Payments
View payments received through your book sales.

Sales Dashboard

The first page you will see is your sales Dashboard. This is a graph charting each sale, borrow and free download of your Kindle book every day. The sales are automatically set for "All marketplaces" and for "All your titles" (if you have more than one book published). You will automatically see the data for the last 30 days. You can specify what time frame you want to look at, as well as specific marketplaces and book titles if you wish. Data can only be displayed as far back as 90 days.

On the graph there are three coloured lines:

- The red line represents every paid sale

- The blue line represents every Kindle Unlimited or Lending Library download

- The green line represents every free download

If you move your curser along one of the lines you will notice small pop-ups that tell you the exact number of sales/downloads on that particular date.

Beneath the graph is a list of royalties earned from each marketplace over the same time period in the graph. Don't forget that the royalties in this chart are reported in the local currency for each marketplace.

Prior Six Weeks Royalties

Shows the royalties you have earned over the previous six weeks. Amazon intend removing this report in the future.

The report is broken down into:

- Week - Date the report refers to

- Title - Title of the book

- Author - Author of the book

- ASIN - Amazon Identification Number for the book

- Units Sold - Number of paid sales

- Units Refunded - Ebooks refunded

- Net Units Sold - Total number of sales minus those refunded

- Royalty Type - Which royalty percentage the book is enrolled on - 35% or 70%

- Transaction Type - Matchbook / Free Price Match / Free Promotion / Countdown / Unlimited / Lending Library / Standard

- Average List Price - Average price your book sold for over the week

- Average File Size - Average file size of your book over the week

- Average Offer Price - Average offer price your book sold for over the week

- Average Delivery Charge - Average delivery charge for your book over the week

- Royalty - Royalties earned during the week

Promotions

This shows a list of the Kindle Countdown Deals you have created. The list shows the marketplace followed by the book name and the date the promotion took place. Click on one of these reports to get detailed information that will include:

- Detail - Increment levels

- List Price - Each incremental price

- Start Time - Start time of each incremental price

- Hours - Number of hours at each price

- Royalty - Percentage royalty earned at each increment

- Royalty / Hour - Royalties earned per hour at each increment

- Compared to Prior Week Average - Compares the royalty per hour during the deal to the previous week

- Total Units - Number of sales at each increment

- Units / Hour - Number of sales at each increment per hour

- Compared to Prior Week Average - Compares the sales per hour during the deal to the previous week

- Revenue - Total revenue at each increment

- Revenue / Hour - Amount of revenue at each increment per hour

- Compared to Prior Week Average - Compares the revenue per hour during the deal to the previous week

Ad Campaigns

This will show you the results of any adverts you have been running. The report is broken down into:

- Status - Whether your campaign is running, ended, or terminated

- Campaign Name - Name of your campaign

- Type - eCommerce

- Start Date - The date your campaign started

- End Date - The date your campaign ended/will end

- Budget - Campaign budget

- Spend - How much your campaign has cost so far

- Impressions - How many times your advert has been shown

- Clicks - How many times your advert has been clicked

- Average CPC - Average cost per click

- Detail Page View - Number of times the page your advert directs a customer to, was viewed

- Total sales - Number of sales as a result of the campaign

Month-To-Date Unit Sales

Click on this and you will see your book sales for each individual marketplace for the current month. Select from the drop down menu a different Amazon marketplace to view data that applies there.

Data is divided up into:

- Title - Title of the book

- ASIN - Amazon Identification Number for the book

- Units Sold - Number of paid sales

- Units Refunded - Ebooks refunded

- Net Units Sold - Total number of sales minus those refunded

- KU/KOLL Units - Number of books downloaded as part of Kindle Unlimited, or borrowed from the lending library

- Free Units-Promo - Number of books downloaded as part of a free promotional deal

- Free Units-Price Match - Number of books downloaded for free after being price matched

Prior Months' Royalties

This shows a summary of the royalties that you earned during the previous month. The list of royalty reports is only supposed to go back for the last 12 months, but it usually displays reports going much further back. Click on the month you would like to look at to download an xls file into your computer. Reports are generated around the 15th day of each month.

When you have downloaded the file you will see various headed columns:

- ASIN - Amazon Identification Number for the book

- Author - Name of the author who wrote the book

- Units Sold - Number of paid sales

- Units Refunded - Ebooks refunded

- Net Units Sold - Total number of sales minus those refunded

- Royalty Type - Which royalty percentage the book is enrolled on - 35% or 70%

- Transaction Type - Matchbook / Free Price Match / Free Promotion / Countdown / Unlimited / Lending Library / Standard

- Average List Price - Average price your book sold for over the month

- Average Offer Price - Average offer price your book sold for over the month

- Average File Size - Average file size of your book over the month

- Average Delivery Cost - Average delivery charge for your book over the month

- Royalty - Royalties earned during the month

Payments

This shows you the royalties you accrued three months previously that has been credited to your bank account It shows the accumulated royalty from each Amazon marketplace as well as its conversion into your local currency. You can change the period of payments that you want to look at as well as which Amazon marketplace and create an Excel report to download to your computer.

The report is broken down into:

- Payment Number - Unique number that identifies that transaction

- Sales Period - Month the sales were generated in

- Marketplace - Which Amazon marketplace the sales were generated in

- Payment Status - Paid / Pending / Failed

- Date - Date the payment was made to your account

- Payment Method - Electronic / Check / Wire

- Accrued Royalty - Total royalties for that sales period in that marketplace

- Tax Withholding - Tax held in the marketplaces local currency

- Adjustments - To correct any previous underpayments, overpayments, refunds. Shown in the marketplaces local currency

- Net Earnings - Royalty amount after tax and adjustments

- FX Rate - Foreign exchange rate applied to your royalties to transfer them into your local currency

- Payment - Final amount paid to you in your local currency

Pre Order Report

See how many pre-order sales and cancellations you have received. You will see a list of books that you have previously had on pre order, as well as those that are due out. Click the title to find out more information.

The report is broken down into:

- Order Date - When the customer pre-ordered the book

- Marketplace - Which Amazon marketplace the pre-order was received

- Pre-Order Units - Number of pre-ordered sales of your book

- Pre-Order Cancellations - Number of cancelled pre-ordered sales of your book

- Pre-Order Units Net of Cancellations - Pre-Order Units minus Cancellations

Excel reports can be downloaded into your computer.

22. Look Inside

When you publish a book through KDP your book will automatically be enrolled on the "Look Inside" facility. This is where potential readers have the opportunity to preview your Kindle book by clicking on the arrow superimposed above your book cover on the marketplace sales page. The "Look Inside" facility is an easy way to get the readers inside your book, read an excerpt of it and hopefully convince them to buy it. "Look Inside" is not always available for printed books but it seems that it is automatically configured after a short wait, especially if your book is published through createspace.com (an Amazon company).

Readers can also get eBook previews sent to their Kindle to read at a later date. When they have read the sample they are also prompted at the end to buy the book to continue reading.

The "Look Inside" function does not currently work on books created using the Amazon's Textbook Creator.

23. Author Central

Author Central is a facility that enables you to create a dedicated author page that lists your books as well as promotional videos, tweets, blog feeds, photographs and a written profile. Author Central allows you to claim all of your own books as well as track various sales data. When readers find one of your books there is a section beneath the reviews entitled "More About the Author" with a brief profile as well as the option to visit the dedicated author page.

More About the Author
› Visit Amazon's Tim Flanagan Page

This option is also available directly beneath the title of the book the reader is looking at. You can see the name of the author with a small arrow in a box beside it. Click the box and an additional window will open that directs readers to your Author Central page.

Tim Flanagan ☑ (Author)

Tim Flanagan (Author)
› Visit Amazon's Tim Flanagan Page
  Find all the books, read about the author, and more.

See search results for this author
Are you an author? Learn about Author Central

At present Author Central is only available on amazon.com, amazon.co.uk, amazon.fr, amazon.de and amazon.jp. To have an Author Central page on these four Amazon websites you need to create four separate Author Central pages that are specific to those marketplaces. You might find that Amazon automatically groups your books, twitter and blog feeds into a semi completed Author Central page on all of the participating marketplaces, but it seems that the photographs and bio do not transfer, so you will need to go into the relevant countries and add the details manually.

How To Set Up Your Amazon.com Author Central Page

For demonstrative purposes, I am going to run through how to set up your Author Central page on amazon.com, however, the same applies to any of the other countries where you wish to complete your Author Central page.

Go to https://authorcentral.amazon.com and click "Join Now" or if you have already signed up just enter the email address and password that is linked to your normal Amazon account.

If you are new to Author Central you will be taken to a Terms & Conditions page, which you will need to agree to before being allowed to move on. You will then need to enter your author name to confirm your identity which will take you to a page that displays all of the authors with a similar name. Click "This is me" beside the book that is yours. You will then receive an email which you will need to confirm by clicking the link.

Your Author Central page allows you add or update information about yourself to populate the page on amazon.com.

Welcome to Author Central

We encourage you to add or update information about yourself for your Amazon Author Page. Here's some quick links to important places:

- **Update your Author Page**
  - Add multimedia, blog feeds, a Twitter feed, or events to an Amazon Author Page
  - View and edit our list of your books
  - Add a book to your bibliography

Build Your Amazon Author page

Beneath the "Update Your Author Page" you will see three bulleted choices. Click on the first option to begin building your Author Page. Any changes that you make to your Author Page could take a while to take effect so you might not see any change immediately.

Add A Biography

Start by adding your biography. Click edit biography to open a new window where you can type in your biography.

Biography   edit biography   delete

Before you write anything, take a look at the guidelines your biography has to adhere to. You can even see a sample biography to give you some ideas. Don't forget that this is a place to write about you, not your books. Try to keep it interesting - this is also being judged by readers as an example of your writing. If it is boring and mundane, readers might assume that your books are the same and be put off buying one. Once it is written click "Preview Biography" to see what it looks like then click "Save Biography" to add it to your page.

Edit biography   close ⊠

Please follow the below guidelines to ensure your submission is acceptable:

- Include a minimum of 100 characters (about 20 words)
- Use plain text only - no rich formatting (bolds, italics) or HTML
- Be creative: share anecdotes or interesting details about yourself with your readers
- See a sample biography ⧉.

Add A Blog Feed

This facility is not available on all the different versions of Author Central.

Every time you write and publish a post on your blog it will automatically be updated onto your Author Central page. Beneath your biography you will see the following section:

Blogs   add blog

Blog Feed   **Status**

Click "Add Blog" to open the window where you can enter the feed from your blog.

Do not just enter the address of your blog. If you are using a wordpress based blog enter the address of your blog followed by /feed so it looks like this - www.yourblog.com/feed. If you are using blogger enter the address of your blog followed by /feeds/posts/default?alt=rss so it will look like this - www.yourblog.com/feeds/posts/default?alt=rss. For other blogs simply click on the blogs RSS icon and you will be taken to your blogs feed address page. Copy the URL and enter it into the box in Author Central.

Finally click "Add" to add it to your page. If you have more than one blog, click "Add Blog" again and enter additional details.

Add Events

This facility is not available on all the different versions of Author Central.

Below the section to add a blog, you have the facility to add events to your page. Click "Add Event" to open the next window.

Events   add event

Manually add in the event information, including a brief description of the event as well as the venue address, date, and time. You can also use the drop down menu to choose which book your event relates to. When you are done click "Save Event". If you have more events you would like to list, just click "Add Event" and complete the form again.

Create Event   close ☒

Description

[   ]

Venue

Begin typing the venue name or address in the boxes below to find your venue. If your
venue does not appear, fill out all the boxes and we'll create this new venue when you save
your event.

Venue Name: [   ]
Street
Address: [   ]
City: [   ]
State/Province: [   ]   Zip/Postal: [   ]
Country: [United States ▼]

Change Venue

Book
[-- Books -- ▼]

Date
Event date: [   ]

Start time: [-- ▼] : [-- ▼] [-- ▼]

[Save event]

Add An Author Page URL

In this section you can add a custom URL to direct people to your
Author Central page. It is easier to own a custom URL that is recognisable,
relevant and memorable, instead of the long page name that will
automatically be assigned to your Author Central page. You can use your
Author Central URL as part of your signature in emails, as well as across all
other social media platforms that you use. You can use up to 30 characters
made from letters, numbers, dashes and underscores but it must contain no
spaces or other special characters. You are limited to only one Author
Central page URL and once you have made it you cannot change it except
by contacting Amazon Customer Services directly. You might find that your
Author Central Page URL has already been taken, if so you will need to
create some sort of variation of the URL to use.

To create your URL click "Add Link" beside the Author Page URL
section on your Author Central page.

Author Page URL   add link ǀ learn more

In the new window that has opened you will see a box which may already have a suggestion for your unique URL. You can delete this if you wish and enter your own variation, or accept what they have suggested. If you enter your own variation Amazon will check to see if it is still available. If it is you will be allowed to click "Save" otherwise you will be instructed that it has already been taken and will need to try another variation. When you are happy click "Save".

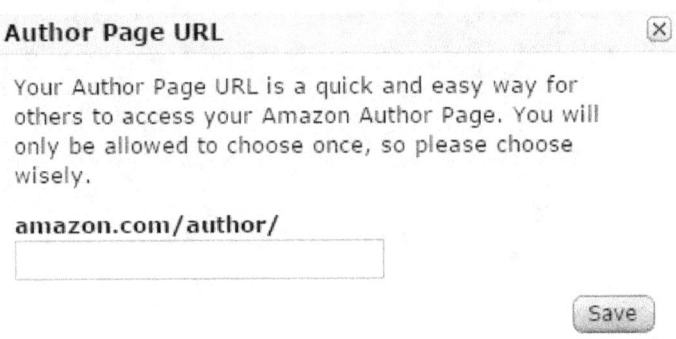

Add Photos

You now have the option to add one or more photographs of yourself.

Click "Add Photo" to begin. In the following window you will be able to upload your photo by clicking "Choose File" where you can select the photo from your computer. You are limited to jpeg, png or gif files that are no more than 4MB in size. They must also be between 300 and 8000 pixels in width and height. Amazon recommend using square pictures of the same height and width. This may mean that you need to resize your photo before you can upload. Once you have selected your photo you must then tick the box confirming that you own or have the rights to use the photo. Click "Upload Photo" to add it to your Author Central page.

Add Photo

Please follow the below guidelines to ensure your submission is acceptable:

- Supported formats include JPEG, PNG, GIF.
- The photo must be between 300 to 8000 pixels in width and height.
- Files must be no more than 4MB.
- We encourage you to feature yourself in your photos, but feel free to add the photos that represent you best as an author.
- See a sample photo ⬈.

Click the browse button below to find photos on your computer

| Choose File | No file chosen |

☐ **I confirm that, as required by the** Terms & Conditions ⬈**, I either own or have cleared all rights to this content and that no further rights or payments are required to distribute it on Amazon properties.**

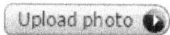

If you want to add another photo just repeat the process. If you only have one photo it will be classed as your main profile image, however if you have more than one you will need to "Manage" your photos. Click "Manage" and you will be able to reorder the photos. Whichever is first will be your main profile image. Or, if you wish to delete one of them, just drag the image below the line. When you have finished click "Save".

Drag and drop photos to reorder them

Drag here to delete

| Cancel | Save |

Add Videos

Add Videos in the same way that you added the photos.

Videos   add video | manage

Click "Add Video" to begin with. In the following window you will be able to upload your video by clicking "Choose File" where you can select it from your oomputer. You **are** limited to avi, flv, mov, mpg, wmv, or mp4 files that are no more than 500MB in size. Once you have selected your video you must then tick the box confirming that you own or have the rights to use it. Click "Upload Video" to add it to your Author Central page.

Add Video

Please follow the below guidelines to ensure your submission is acceptable:

- Supported formats include AVI, FLV, MOV, MPG, WMV, MP4.
- Files must be smaller than 500MB.
- For more guidelines, please visit our video content guidelines ⬈.

Click the browse button below to find videos on your computer

Choose File | No file chosen

☐ **I confirm that, as required by the** Terms & Conditions ⬈, **I either own or have cleared all rights to this content and that no further rights or payments are required to distribute it on Amazon properties.**

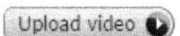

If you want to add another video just repeat the process. If you only have the one video this will be classed as your main video, however if you have more than one you will need to "Manage" your videos. Click "Manage" and you will be able to reorder the videos. Whichever is first will be classed as your main video. Or, if you wish to delete one of them, just drag the video below the line. When you have finished click "Save".

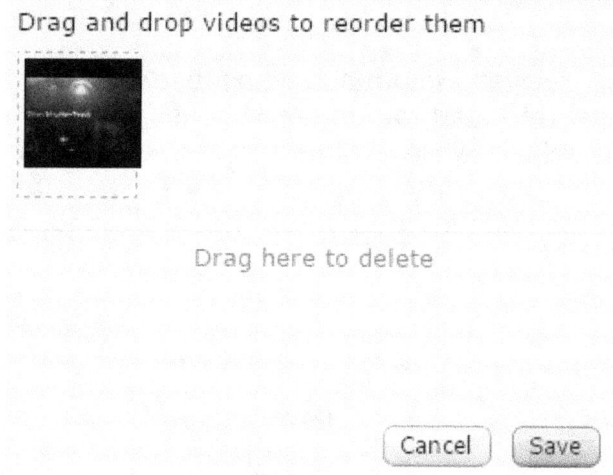

Add A Twitter Feed

Finally for this section you need to add in your Twitter feed.

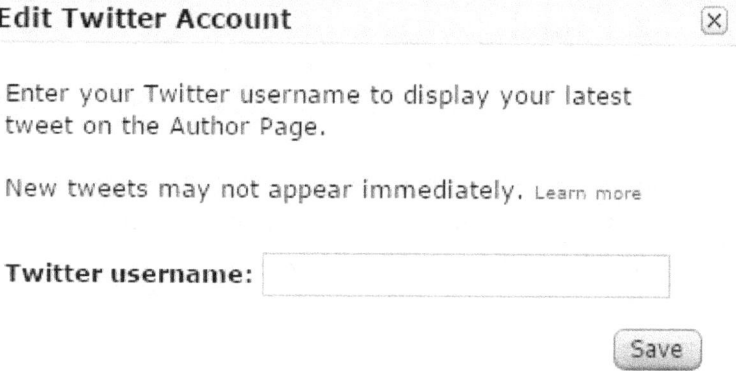

Click "Edit Account" to open up a new window where you can add your Twitter username into the available space. Make sure the username is exactly as it is in Twitter without spaces and without the @ symbol. Once you have completed this, click "Save".

Add Your books

Now that the relevant information has been added to your Author Central page you need to start to add your books. When you have selected your books it might take a while for them to appear in your Author Central Page on Amazon.

At the top of the Author Page you will see a menu, click the second option - "Books".

amazon Author Central   Author Page   **Books**   Sales Info ⌄   Customer Reviews

This will take you to a different page where you can claim the books that are yours. You will see a button inviting you to "Add Books" or, if you have already added one, it might say "Add More Books".

Add more books

Click this button to open a new window where you can enter details of either the title, author or ISBN number of the book you are searching for. Click "Go" and Amazon will search its database for all of the possible books that might be relevant to your search. When you see your book click the "This is my book" button.

This is my book

That book will be added to your page, but might take a short time to appear. Once it does you will see it listed in the "Books" tab beneath the "Add more books" button.

Sales Information

At the top of the Author Central Page you will see the option "Sales Info" on the menu. Click this to see a dropdown menu with three options.

amazon
Author Central   Author Page   **Books**   Sales Info ˅   Customer Reviews

Nielsen BookScan

Sales Rank

Author Rank

Nielsen BookScan

This data is only available on your amazon.com version of Author Central. This is the sales information concerning the number of print books you have sold across the US in the past 4 weeks. Sales figures are gathered from Amazon, Barnes & Noble, Deseret Book Company, Hastings, Target, Follett College stores and Buy.com, but do not include sales by Wal-Mart, to libraries, of used books, or those published through Createspace.

Books published through Createspace might get included in these figures if you have selected the Expanded Distribution Channel when you published through them. Because most self published authors use print on demand websites to produce a print version of their book, the data you will get from the Nielsen BookScan is limited and not necessarily accurate.

Kindle and other eBook sales are not included in Nielsen BookScan. Nielsen admit that only about 75% of print book sales in the US are reported in the BookScan.

The highlights at the top of the page give you a summary of your print sales. You can see the sales of your print book by State by clicking on the "Sales by Geography" option on the left side. For more accurate sales data for self published authors on your printed books, go to the print on demand platform you used to publish your book and obtain exact figures from there.

Sales Rank

Click on this tab and you will see all of your books listed beside a graph showing the ranking of the book over time. You will also see the current rank number and how that has changed since yesterday. The ranking figures are updated hourly. If you want more detailed information about one particular book, click on its title to see a larger graph.

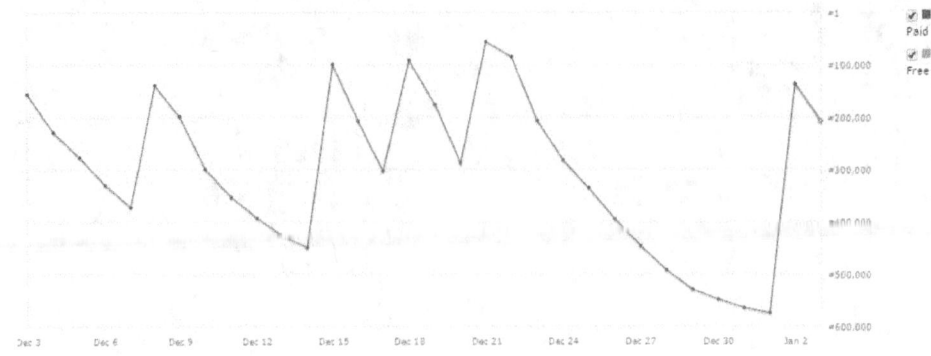

You can change the period of time for the data you want to see by selecting 2 weeks, 1 month, or all available. Each day represents a dot on the graph. If you run a free promotion you will notice an orange line in your graph indicating where it appeared in the free rankings. You can gain information for each individual book in print and Kindle formats which you can then compare with any specific sales promotion and marketing to see if it resulted in a peak in sales. Don't forget that these are the sales ranks only for your books in the specific country relevant to the Author Central page you are working on.

Author Rank

This facility is not available on all the different versions of Author Central.

Author Rank is slightly different to your Sales Rank. Whereas Sales Rank concerns each individual book, your Author Rank is how you rank alongside other authors. To determine this Amazon takes the sales of all your Kindle and print books and compares it with other authors sales. The Author Rank appears on your book sales pages if you rank in the overall top 100. In the sales information tab on your Author Central Page you will see that your ranking is plotted in graph form in exactly the same way as the Sales Rank is.

On both the Sales Rank and the Author Rank you can narrow down your specific rankings according to the categories your books are listed in, or just Kindle sales, or just print sales. The ranking you see when you click through to the pages is your overall ranking taking into account all sales, all books, all formats, all categories. Don't forget that this is the Author Rank in the specific country relevant to the Author Central page you are working on.

Customer Reviews

The final tab in the Author Central menu shows you your most recent reviews all in one place.

amazon
Author Central   Author Page   Books   Sales Info ⌄   **Customer Reviews**

By clicking the "Customer Reviews" tab you will be able to read the most recent reviews that customers have left about your books.

24. Kindle Singles

Kindle Singles are novels that don't typically fall into the categories for normal books. They are between 5,000 and 30,000 words long and can be written about any topic that is interesting and compelling. Amazon have published a variety of books as Kindle Singles including fiction, essays, memoirs, reports, and narratives.

Kindle Singles feature in their own listing on Amazon together with their own categories, but that doesn't mean they won't also feature in the normal Bestseller listings as well. There are a lot less new titles being published in the Kindle Singles chart than the normal marketplace so you have a much greater chance of being noticed if your book falls into the required criteria.

< Kindle Store

Kindle Singles

Arts & Entertainment (66)

At Play (39)

Essays & Ideas (117)

Fiction (169)

History (76)

Humor (39)

Memoirs (115)

Page-turning Narratives (119)

Profiles (64)

Pulp Nonfiction (25)

Reporting (131)

Society (114)

The Kindle Singles
Interview (14)

The Latest (44)

The Sciences (43)

The World Stage (101)

Kindle Singles en Español (9)

To be included in the Kindle Singles chart you will need to manually submit your book to Amazon. Authors can still request the 70% royalty option even for titles sold below the $2.99 threshold.

Submission Criteria

If you wish to submit your book it will need to fit the following criteria:

- Between 5,000 and 30,000 words long

- Priced between $0.99 and $4.99

- Unpublished, or self published on KDP, or a book idea proposal

- Not part of a series

- Not preview chapters from a bigger piece of work

- Not a How-To Manual, Reference book, travel guide or children's book

- Not a collections of stories

- You must hold all rights to the book

- Cannot contain public domain material

How To Submit

For books that are already self published on KDP:

Email Amazon at kindle-singles@amazon.com including the following:

- Cover letter

- Book Title

- Book ASIN

- Summary of the book

For books that are written, but not yet published:

Email Amazon at kindle-singles@amazon.com including the following:

- Cover letter

- Manuscript of the book

- Your name

For book proposal ideas:

Email Amazon at kindle-singles@amazon.com including the following:

- Cover letter

- Proposal of the book

- Your name

Once you have contacted Amazon with the relevant information it will be reviewed by their editors and you should receive a reply within six weeks with instructions on how to publish the book as a Kindle Single.

25. Kindle Worlds

At the moment Kindle Worlds is only available to readers in the USA, although authors outside the US can still submit their books for inclusion they will only be available to buy on amazon.com.

Kindle Worlds can be accessed by going to https://kindleworlds.amazon.com/ and signing in with your Amazon log in details.

Kindle Worlds is a place where you can submit stories that are based on already established worlds that other writers have created. These worlds include those created for successful book series, as well as television series and characters. If approved, your story will be made available on amazon.com and you will receive royalties on it, but you will also gain the additional exposure of linking your book to already successful authors and series.

Each world has their own set of guidelines and rules which your book will also need to adhere to if you want to submit it for inclusion. Once you have chosen a world, you can submit your story.

Your submission should be:

- A text only novels (illustrated stories are not currently accepted)

- 5,000 words or more

- Written in English

- Word doc, RTF or TXT file format

- Cover Image

- Must be exclusive to Kindle Worlds

Once your novel has been submitted, Kindle Worlds will review it before publication to make sure that it follows the relevant "World Content Guidelines", and provides a quality reader experience. You should hear within two days if you have been successful.

If successful your book will be made available on amazon.com, as well as at the Kindle Worlds store. The list price for your book will be set between $0.99 and $3.99. For works of 10,000 words or more you will receive 35% royalty rate. Books 5,000 - 9,999 words will receive 20% royalties. As with normal self publishing guidelines, royalties are paid monthly, sixty days after the end of the month that the royalties were accrued.

26. Amazon Marketing

Recently Amazon gave authors the opportunity to create sales campaigns to help promote their books to customers on amazon.com. Authors can create an ad campaign regardless where they live, however the advert will only be seen on amazon.com.

Amazon marketing is only available for books that are enrolled on KDP Select. It doesn't cost anything to register for Amazon Marketing, but you are charged on a cost-per-click basis on your advert.

If you already have a KDP account you can access the advertising campaign by going to your "Bookshelf" in your KDP account. Choose the book you would like to promote and beneath the column titled "KDP Select" you will see the "Promote and Advertise" option.

If you are using the new version "Bookshelf", select the options box on the far right beside the relevant book and in the opening window select "Promote and Advertise".

Edit Details

Edit Rights, Royalty, and Pricing

KDP Select Info

Promote and Advertise

Edit Matchbook

Unpublish

Clicking on this will take you through to another page that gives you the option to run a Free Book Promotion or Kindle Countdown Deal, however, on the right of the screen is the option for running an ad campaign.

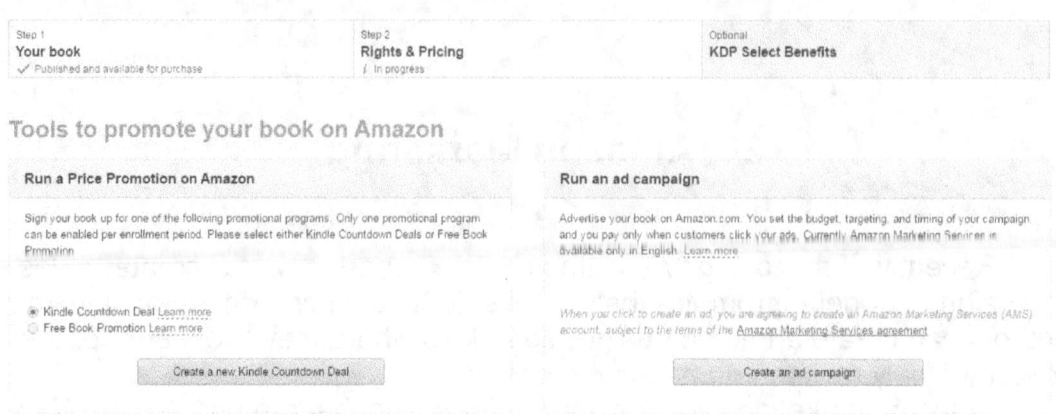

Click on "Create an ad campaign". In the page that opens you have the choice to select which book you would like to create a campaign for.

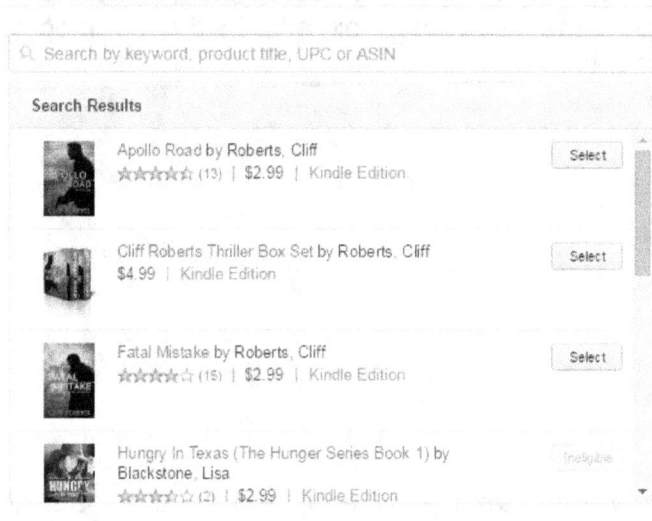

Click the "Select" button beside the book you wish to promote. If you want to promote more than one book, you will need to set up a separate advertising campaign for each one. Once you have selected the book you then need to choose how you want to target your audience.

Target Your Ad

Target Your Ad

◯ By product
Show your ad to customers interested in selected and similar products.

◯ By interest
Show your ad to customers interested in selected categories.

By product:

You will be given the opportunity to choose specific products that potential customers of your book might also be looking at. This is very specific targeting that will result in less impressions, but a more successful click through rate.

Once you have selected this option you will be asked to search for products similar to yours. Type in a keyword, phrase or product in the search bar and Amazon will automatically show you up to 146 results. You can add each individual product to your campaign, or click "Add all on this page" for all of the results on that page (up to 30 will be shown at a time) to be included. Press the forward arrow to see the next batch of 30 results and add as you wish. Keep going until you have viewed all of the search results. You can stop at that if you want to, or type in additional products and add them to the campaign. There doesn't appear to be any limit to the number of products you can add.

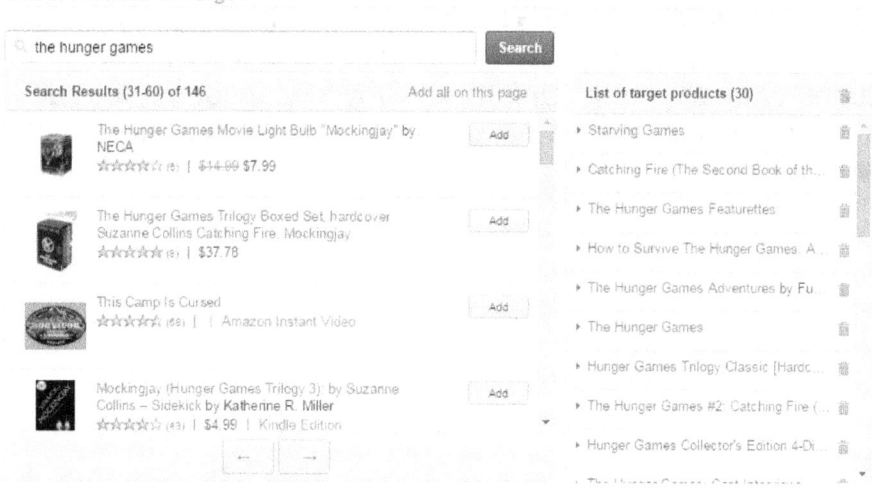

As you add target products to your campaign you will see them included on a separate list beside the search results. You can remove any of them by clicking the "Trash" button beside the product. You will notice that there is a tick box option beneath the search results. To increase the number of impressions Amazon will also promote your book beside other products that closely match the ones you have added to your campaign list. You can choose whether or not you want Amazon to do this on your behalf.

By interest:

If you know the categories that your customers enjoy you can choose this option. Categories are more broader options for your target audience and will result in a lot more impressions, but a lower click through rate.

Once you have selected this option you will see a list of shopper interests. Click one to add it to your campaign list.

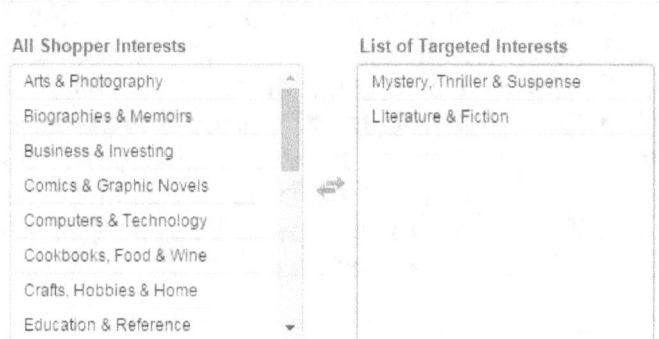

You can choose as many as you wish. If you decide to remove one, just click it in the "List of Targeted Interests" box and it will return back to the "All Shopper Interests" box. Unfortunately you cannot narrow down the interests any more than the list Amazon provides, so you will be seen by a very broad audience.

Set Your Campaign Name, Bid and Budget

Set your campaign name, bid and budget

Campaign name	My Book Campaign

Cost-per-click bid (CPC)	$	0.05
	Recommended CPC bid is 0.05	

Budget	$	100.00
	Minimum budget is $100	

Clicks and impressions are not guaranteed. How will my budget be spent? ▾

Once you have decided who to target you need to give your campaign a name so that you can easily identify it when you're looking at the results in your KDP reports. You will also need to decide what the maximum cost will be that you are willing to spend on each click (CPC). Your campaign will only be charged every time someone clicks on the ad and goes through to your book page. Amazon recommend a cost of $0.05 per click, but you can bid higher if you wish. Every single advert that you are competing against is set in an auction for that space, so you could pay less than the CPC you choose, but never more. If you decide to spend more on your CPC you are probably going to get more impressions which could result in more click throughs. However, you need to think carefully about what your CPC is going to be and base it on the royalty you would receive if the click successfully resulted in a sale. You will also need to set your budget. The minimum budget is set at $100, but don't worry, you don't need to spend all of that. If you find a campaign is not working you can terminate it so that it doesn't eat into that $100. Amazon will only bill you for the click throughs your campaign receives.

Campaign Settings

Campaign Settings

Duration From today until 05/12/2015

Pacing Deliver my campaign as quickly as possible ⊙

⌄ Edit campaign settings

Amazon will automatically set your campaign to run for a duration of a month from the day you create it. They will also try and complete your campaign as quickly as possible, spending your budget before the end of the month's campaign. But you can change all of this by clicking "Edit campaign settings".

Campaign Settings

Start date 04/12/2015 📅   **End date** 05/12/2015 📅

Pacing ⦿ Deliver my campaign as quickly as possible ⊙
⊙ Allow Amazon to spread out my campaign smoothly ⊙

Now you can choose when you want your campaign to start and end, as well as having the option of spreading the cost of your campaign out evenly throughout the duration. If you choose this option the same percentage of your budget will be spent every day until the end of the campaign. Allowing your campaign to be delivered as quickly as possible enables you to capitalize on any sudden surges of interest in particular products or categories that might drive sales, so you take advantage of fluctuations in the market, but it could use up your budget quicker.

Preview Your Ad

You can now see how your ad will look in various size formats depending on where it will be displayed on the Amazon marketplace pages. Some readers will even see your book on their eReader in the form of a screensaver or advertised on their home page.

Payment Settings

Select how you are going to pay for your campaign. Click "Add a card" to enter your credit or debit card information.

Once everything has been completed, click "Submit campaign for review". You will need to wait for Amazon to approve your ad campaign. Once they have you will receive an email from them and your campaign will immediately go live, or scheduled to go live if you chose a later date.

You can review the performance of your ad campaigns in the reports section of your KDP dashboard.

If you want to change the settings of a campaign, open your "Ad Campaigns" option from the report page of your KDP account and select the campaign you wish to change. On the "Campaign Settings" tab you can change the CPC, budget and duration of your campaign. If you click on the "Targeting" tab you can delete products or categories and add others.

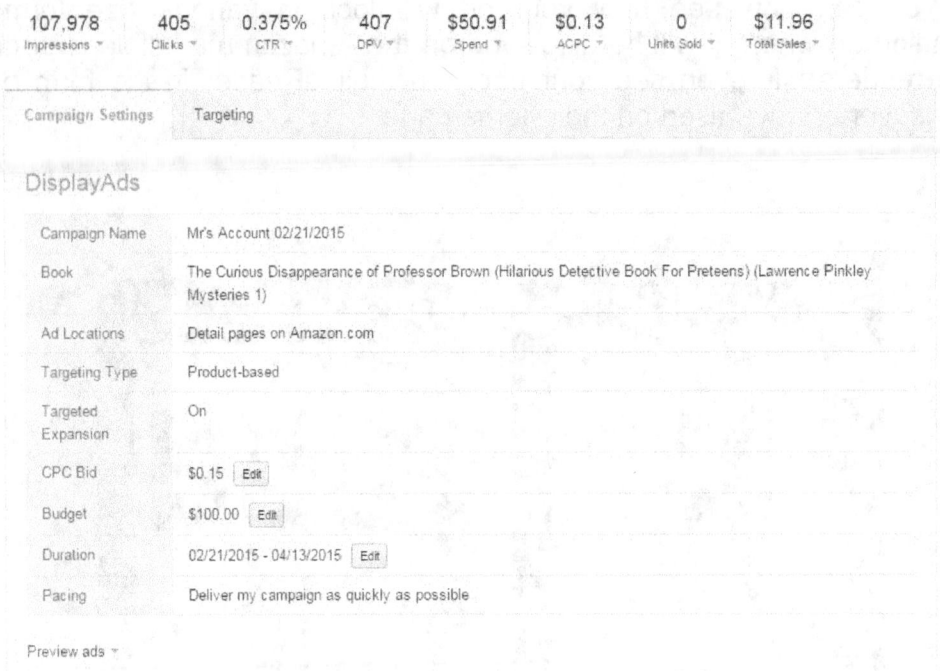

Sponsored search campaigns and keyword data is not currently available to authors.

27. Price Matching

Amazon have a policy of price matching which will effect the price they sell your book at, even if you have chosen to sell it at a particular price when you completed the Book Details Page in KDP. Prices of the same book on other platforms are automatically checked and Amazon will consistently try to make their prices more competitive.

If your book is price matched it will not effect your royalty option. For example if your book was enrolled in the 70% royalty option and it is reduced in price to match a competitor you will still receive 70% of the final list price.

Using Price Matching To Create A Permafree Book

Permafree is when your book is permanently free rather than just the 5 day period when you are participating in a free promotional deal through KDP Select. You might want to have a permanently free book as a way of tempting readers into a series of books. Hopefully customers will like what they read and purchase the other books in the series. But the minimum price you can set your book at in the KDP Book Details Page is $0.99 on the 35% royalty option, so how can you get it to be free forever?

To start with you must remove your book from KDP Select so your book is not exclusive to Amazon. Then go onto a rivals website such as Nook, Kobo, or iTunes and upload your eBook to their stores and set the price of the book to free. Give it a little time for everything to filter into place. Once your book is free at one of the other stores you need to inform Amazon. You can do this by going to your book's sales page and scrolling down to the Product Details section. Just below that you will see one line that asks for feedback on images or informing them of a lower price.

Would you like to **give feedback on images** or **tell us about a lower price**?

Click "tell us about a lower price" and you will be asked where you saw the lower price. Check the tab beside "Website" and add the URL and price then click "Submit Feedback".

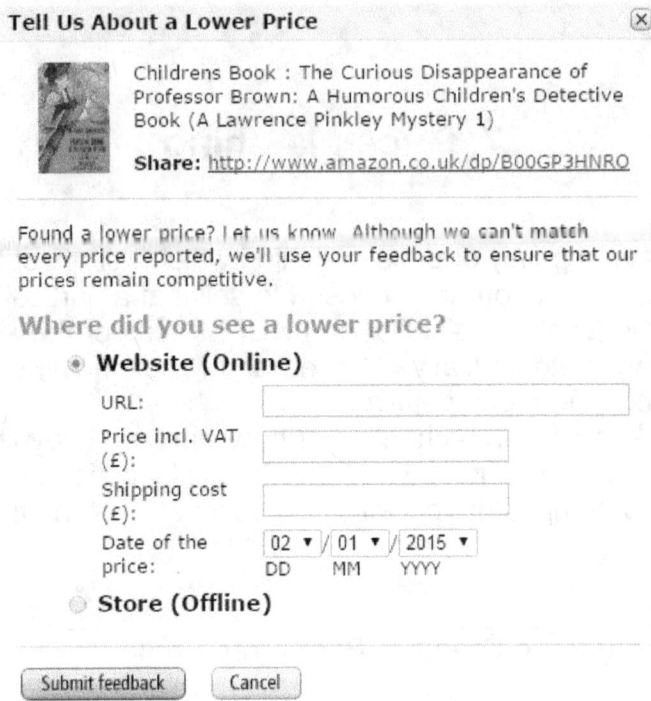

If your book is available on several other online stores, it can't do any harm completing the form again with the other retailers information. You won't see anything happen for a while but if nothing has changed after two weeks it would be a good idea to complete the lower price forms again or get a friend to do the same for you.

Once your book is priced free you need to check it regularly to make sure that it does not revert back to the original price. If it does, submit the lower price feedback again. Don't forget you cannot enrol that book in the KDP Select scheme and that book cannot participate in Kindle Unlimited or promotional schemes whilst it is being price matched.

28. Amazon Cart

Amazon cart is a new service from Amazon who have teamed up directly with Twitter to enable Twitter users to add products to their shopping cart on Amazon without having to leave Twitter. When you see something that you want to buy, just reply to the tweet with #amazoncart and it will automatically be added to your cart for you to purchase later.

You can also use this same system to get customers on Twitter to add products to their wishlist by replying to a product tweet with #amazonwishlist. The conversion rate of products added to a wishlist may be lower than if they have automatically been added to a shopping cart.

#amazoncart will not work if your Twitter account is protected. Your account must be set to public. When you reply with #amazoncart you have not purchased the item, merely added it to your cart which you can edit or delete at a later time. You will receive a reply tweet from @myamazon confirming whether the item was successfully added to your cart and how to check out later.

This can be a useful tool when promoting your books. Impulsive buys via Twitter without the customer having to leave the social media platform could increase your sales, especially during a promotional period.

How Readers Can Set Up Amazon Cart

Amazon cart will only work if customers have connected their Amazon account to their Twitter account. Encourage people to do this by sending them to:

http://www.amazon.com/gp/socialmedia/amazoncart/ref=amazoncart_surl_a mazoncartlp

...and click "Get Started".
Amazon will ask for your permission to install the app:

Click "Authorize App" if you are happy to continue then sign in to your Amazon account as normal.

You will then receive confirmation that your Amazon and Twitter accounts are linked.

29. Amazon Associates

If you have a blog or website that features your books (or other peoples) you can earn additional income by participating in Amazon Associates where you will earn money (up to 10%) by referring customers to Amazon who then subsequently go on to buy something.

Amazon Associates is an easy way to earn extra income on your book sales to top up your royalties.

Setting Up Your Account

To set up an Amazon Associates account, just click on the "Amazon Associates" button you can see at the top right of an Amazon store page and click join. Sign in with your Amazon account details.

Once you have confirmed your personal details you will be taken through to a new page where Amazon ask you for more information about the website and products you intend to promote. Once these pages have been completed Amazon will need verify your identity. Enter your phone number along with your international dialling code to receive an electronic message giving you your PIN number. You will see a space on the computer screen where you can enter this PIN number. Once you have done that you will need to tick to agree to the terms and conditions and click "Finish".

You will now be able to set up the associate links that you can use in your blog. However, before you do that you will need to complete the payment and tax information forms.

Your Payment Method

Choose how you want to be paid from the following options:

- Get paid by amazon.com gift certificate/card

- Get paid by direct deposit (US Associates only)

- Get paid by check (fees apply)

You will then need to complete the tax forms which will be depend on whether you are a US citizen or not.

If you are a US Citizen:
Amazon will take the information you have already completed (name and address) to complete the relevant form. Make sure it is accurate and matches exactly what details you complete for your US Income Tax Returns. You will need to select what Federal Tax Classification you fall into, as well as supplying your Tax Identification Number (TIN), including your Social Security Number (SSN - found on your Social Security Card) or Individual Tax Identification Number (ITIN - on the CP565 notice from IRS) or Employer Identification Number (EIN - on the CP575A notice from IRS).

This data is then used to complete your W-9 form. Review this information to make sure it is accurate then click "Save" to continue to the next page.

Amazon will then need to provide an electronic version of your tax information reporting form 1099-MISC to the IRS, but require your consent. You will be able to obtain an electronic version of this form on or before January 31st each year. If you do not provide consent Amazon will mail a printed copy to the address you provided.

The next part is to consent to Form W-9. This can be done electronically, but if you prefer, you can print the form and send a signed copy to Amazon at: Amazon, Attn: Vendor Maintenance, PO Box 80683, Seattle, WA 98108-0683, USA.

Double check all information, particularly your name and TIN before submitting

If you are a non US citizen:
You need to define what type of beneficial owner you are. Most self published people will be classed as an individual. Complete your country of citizenship and your name as it appears on your tax return. Amazon will use the information you have already completed (name and address) for some parts of this form. You will need to declare whether you hold a valid US Green Card or have spent 31 days during the current year, or 183 days during the previous three year period in the US.

Declare if you have a US Tax Identification Number (TIN). Most self published authors who live outside of the US will need to check the box declaring you do not have a US TIN or foreign Income Tax Identification Number. This data is put into your W-8 Form. Review this information to make sure it is accurate then click "Save" to continue to the next page.

Amazon need to provide an electronic version of your tax information reporting form 1042-S to the IRS, but require your consent. You will be able to obtain an electronic version of this form on or before March 15th each year. If you do not provide consent Amazon will mail a printed copy to the address you provided.

The next part is to consent to Form W-8. This can be done electronically, but if you prefer, you can print the form and send a signed copy to Amazon at: Amazon, Attn: Vendor Maintenance, PO Box 80683, Seattle, WA 98108-0683, USA.

Double check all information, before submitting the forms.

Creating Links

In the main associate page you will see a search bar.

Welcome to Associates Central

Quickly Add Links

Search for a product   **Browse for a product**

keyword or ASIN/ISBN   advanced search

Enter the name of the book you wish to acquire associate earnings from and you will see all the results displayed beneath it including print and Kindle formats as separate results. Beside the product you want you will see a box that says "Get Link". Click that to see the code for that product. This is the code you need to attach as a hyperlink to the product in your blog. So, if it was your book you would hyperlink the image of your book in your blog with this code. When a customer clicks through from your blog Amazon will know where they have come from and if that customer buys something on that visit you will earn money from it.

Copy and paste the link below | Shorten URL with amzn.to?

http://www.amazon.com/gp/product/B00M4OB694/ref=as_li_qf
_sp_asin_il_tl?
ie=UTF8&camp=1789&creative=9325&creativeASIN=B00M4OB694&

Highlight HTML   Build more links

Click "Highlight HTML" then right click and copy. Open up your blog admin and paste the link where you want it.

30. Adjusting Your Book Details

Once your book has been published that doesn't mean you stop using Amazon. Change your book details regularly to reflect changing marketing patterns. There is no restriction on the number of times you can change your books details, the only thing you will have to do is wait for your alterations to be approved which can take 12 hours if it is an English written book or up to 48 hours for a non-English book. Whilst waiting for any alterations to be approved, your book will still be available for buyers to see online but without the updated information.

Updating Your Book Description

You may occasionally want to update the book description to include new positive or high profile book reviews, add to your book list if it increases, incorporate changes in keywords to make it more discoverable, improve the book description or html tag appearance.

Update The Contents Of The Book

There may be several times you might want to adjust the internal contents of your book. If a reviewer found a spelling mistake, you can easily change it and re-upload to KDP. You might also want to alter the front matter. Maybe you had some great reviews - put small bites of the review on the front page. Also, if you have released a new book, don't forget to list it at the front of your old books. It might also be good to include the first chapter of a new book at the end of your old book. Just because you have finished writing the book and published it, doesn't mean you leave it alone. Keep improving wherever you can.

Update Series Title

If you write a second book that forms part of a series, don't forget to go back to the first book and complete the relevant field so that both books will be labelled on the product page as being from the same series.

Updating Sub Title

Change the subtitle occasionally to incorporate new keywords or phrases to see if it helps with sales.

Change The Price

Change the price by scheduling Kindle Countdown Deals or Free Promotional Deals, or adjust the price manually when you have a promotion running. If you have written another book in the same series, go back and alter the price of the first book to make it more appealing and tempting as a way of drawing readers into the series.

Adjust The Categories

If the categories you are listed in are getting a bit crowded or your ranking within that category is dropping it may be worth changing categories. Also research the sub categories and decide whether changing the sub category keywords would be worthwhile.

Adjusting Keywords

This is the part of your book details that you might change most regularly. If you are using keywords that relate to current products and trends then they will need updating at least once a week.

Expand Author Central

As you write more books, don't forget to claim them in your Author Central page. You might also want to update your bio occasionally, add new events, and add any new video trailers that you have created. It is important to keep your Author Central page up to date - this is your shop window in Amazon.

31. Kindle Scout

This facility is currently only available to authors in the USA.

Kindle Scout is a system where authors can place there never-before-published books and let readers decide if they get published or not. Once your book has been submitted and approved, readers will get 30 days to nominate your book for the chance to be published by Kindle Press.

If your Kindle Scout campaign is successful the book will be reviewed by Kindle Press. If published you will receive a $1,500 advance, 50% eBook royalty rate and featured Amazon marketing. A Kindle Press contract is renewable every five years and only applies to eBook and audio formats. You will still be able to publish print editions through other publishers or self publishing. Royalties are paid monthly, 30 days after the end of the month in which the sales occurred. Kindle Press will price your book between $2.99 and $4.99 although they reserve the right to change it according to market fluctuations. Books published by Kindle Press will also be enrolled in Kindle Owners' Lending Library and Kindle Unlimited. They will be promoted through targeted email campaigns and promotions. If a book published with Kindle Press doesn't earn $25,000 in royalties during the five year term, the author can choose to stop publishing with Kindle Press.

For your book to be eligible for submission you must adhere to the following criteria:

- You must be over 18 years old

- Must have a valid US bank account and US Social Security number

- The book must be in one of the following genres: Romance, Mystery and Thriller, Science Fiction and Fantasy, and Literature and Fiction. Action and Adventure Contemporary Fiction and Historical Fiction are accepted within the Literature and Fiction category

- Your book must never have been published before

- It must be your own work

- Must be 50,000 words or more

- In "Word" format

- Must be of the highest standard

- The content and cover image must not be offensive - no racial slurs, pornography or offensive depictions of sex, or excessively violent material

- Must be written in English

- Must be the work of a single author

Once you have submitted your book it will be put before a team of reviewers who will decide whether to approve the book or not. You should hear the outcome within 1-2 business days.

You can only submit one book at a time. You cannot publish the book anywhere else for 45 days after you submit it to Kindle Scout. The first 5,000 words of your book will be shown to the public as an excerpt of your book. It is based on this that readers will decide whether to nominate you or not.

Submitting To Kindle Scout

If you feel you are ready to submit your work, go to the "Submit Your Book" page at https://kindlescout.amazon.com/submit

As well as your manuscript, you will also need to submit the following information:

- Book title

- Book cover image - jpeg or png file format. File must be no larger than 5MB and 4500pixels x 2820 pixels in size

- One liner - 45 characters or less

- Book description - 500 characters or less

- Your bio - 500 characters or less

- Author photo

- You will be asked to answer three author based questions about yourself and the book

- Thank you note - 500 characters or less. This is the note that readers will receive if they nominate your book

If your submission is unsuccessful you might need to revise the content of your book. However, if your book has been accepted you will receive an email from Kindle Scout confirming that your campaign has been launched. Contact your social media followers and email subscribers and direct them to the page that shows your book and get them to support you.

At the end of the campaign, if your book has been successful you might get selected for publication by Kindle Press. You will then have 30 days to finalize your manuscript and cover image, and provide banking details. All readers who nominated your book will receive a free copy if successfully published.

APPENDICES

Appendix A
Categories - Fiction

General
Action & Adventure
African American
- ➲ General
- ➲ Christian
- ➲ Contemporary Women
- ➲ Erotica
- ➲ Historical
- ➲ Mystery & Detective
- ➲ Urban
Alternative History
Amish & Mennonite
Anthologies
Asian American
Biographical
Christian
- ➲ General
- ➲ Classic & Allegory
- ➲ Collections & Anthologies
- ➲ Fantasy
- ➲ Futuristic
- ➲ Historical
- ➲ Romance
- ➲ Suspense
- ➲ Western
Classics
Coming of age
Contemporary Women
Crime
Cultural Heritage
Dystopian
Erotica
Fairy Tales, Folk Tales, Legends & Mythology
Family Life
Fantasy
- ➲ General
- ➲ Collections & Anthologies

- ➲ Contemporary
- ➲ Dark Fantasy
- ➲ Epic
- ➲ Historical
- ➲ Paranormal
- ➲ Urban
Gay
Ghost
Gothic
Hispanic & Latino
Historical
Holidays
Horror
Humorous
Jewish
Legal
Lesbian
Literary
Mashups
Media Tie-In
Medical
Mystery & Detective
- ➲ General
- ➲ Collections & Anthologies
- ➲ Cozy
- ➲ Hard-Boiled
- ➲ Historical
- ➲ International Mystery & Crime
- ➲ Police Procedural
- ➲ Private Investigators
- ➲ Traditional British
- ➲ Woman Sleuths
Native American & Aboriginal
Occult & Supernatural
Political
Psychological
Religious

Romance
- General
- African American
- Collections & Anthologies
- Contemporary
- Erotica
- Fantasy
- Historical
    - General
    - Ancient World
    - Medieval
    - Regency
    - Scottish
    - Victorian
    - Viking
- Paranormal
- Science Fiction
- Suspense
- Time Travel
- Western

Sagas
Satire
Science Fiction
- General
- Action & adventure

- Apocalyptic & Post-Apocalyptic
- Collections & Anthologies
- Hard Science Fiction
- Military
- Space Opera
- Steampunk
- Time Travel

Sea Stories
Short Stories
Sports
Thrillers
- General
- Crime
- Espionage
- Historical
- Legal
- Medical
- Military
- Political
- Suspense
- Technological

Urban
Visionary & Metaphysical
War & Military
Westerns

Appendix B
Categories - Juvenile Fiction

General
Action & Adventure
➲ General
➲ Pirates
➲ Survival Stories
Activity Books
Animals
➲ General
➲ Alligators & Crocodiles
➲ Apes, Monkeys, etc
➲ Baby Animals
➲ Bears
➲ Birds
➲ Butterflies, Moths & Caterpillars
➲ Cats
➲ Cows
➲ Deer, Moose & Caribou
➲ Dinosaurs & Prehistoric Creatures
➲ Dogs
➲ Dragons, Unicorns & Mythical
➲ Duck, Geese, etc
➲ Elephants
➲ Farm Animals
➲ Fishes
➲ Foxes
➲ Frogs & Toads
➲ Giraffes
➲ Hippos & Rhinos
➲ Horses
➲ Insects, Spiders, etc
➲ Jungle Animals
➲ Kangaroos
➲ Lions, Tigers, Leopards, etc
➲ Mammals
➲ Marine Life

➲ Mice, Hamsters, Guinea Pigs, etc
➲ Nocturnal
➲ Pets
➲ Pigs
➲ Rabbits
➲ Reptiles & Amphibians
➲ Squirrels
➲ Turtles
➲ Wolves & Coyotes
➲ Zoos
Art & Architecture
Bedtime & Dreams
Biographical
➲ General
➲ Canada
➲ European
➲ Other
➲ United States
Books & Libraries
Boys & Men
Business, Careers, Occupations
Classics
Clothing & Dress
Comics & Graphic Novels
➲ General
➲ Manga
➲ Media Tie-In
➲ Superheroes
Computers
Concepts
➲ General
➲ Alphabet
➲ Body
➲ Colors
➲ Counting & Numbers
➲ Date & Time
➲ Money

- Opposites
- Seasons
- Senses & Sensation
- Size & Shape
- Sounds
- Words

Cooking & Food
Dystopian
Fairy Tales & Folklore
- General
- Adaptations
- Anthologies
- Country & Ethnic

Family
- General
- Adoption
- Alternative Family
- Marriage & Divorce
- Multigenerational
- New Baby
- Orphans & Foster Homes
- Parents
- Siblings
- Stepfamilies

Fantasy & Magic
Gay & Lesbian
Girls & Women
Health & Daily Living
- General
- Daily Activities
- Diseases, Illnesses & Injuries
- Toilet Training

Historical
- General
- African
- Ancient Civilizations
- Asia
- Canada
  - General
  - Post-Confederation
  - Pre-Confederation
- Europe
- Exploration & Discovery
- Holocaust
- Medieval

- Middle East
- Military & Wars
- Other
- Prehistory
- Renaissance
- United States
  - General
  - 19th Century
  - 20th Century
  - 21st Century
  - Civil War Period
  - Colonial & Revolutionary Periods

Holidays & Celebrations
- General
- Birthdays
- Christmas & Advent
- Easter & Lent
- Halloween
- Hanukkah
- Kwanzaa
- Other, Non-Religious
- Other, Religious
- Passover
- Patriotic Holidays
- Thanksgiving
- Valentine's Day

Horror & Ghost Stories
Humorous Stories
Imagination & Play
Interactive Adventures
Law & Crime
Legends, Myths, Fables
- General
- Arthurian
- Greek & Roman
- Norse
- Other

Lifestyles
- City & Town Life
- Country Life
- Farm & Ranch Life

Love & Romance
Media Tie-In
Monsters
Mysteries & Detective Stories

Nature & the Natural World
- ⮑ General
- ⮑ Environment
- ⮑ Weather

Nursery Rhymes

Paranormal

People & Places
- ⮑ General
- ⮑ Africa
- ⮑ Asia
- ⮑ Australia & Oceania
- ⮑ Canada
  - ⮑ General
  - ⮑ Native Canadian
- ⮑ Caribbean & Latin America
- ⮑ Europe
- ⮑ Mexico
- ⮑ Middle East
- ⮑ Other
- ⮑ Polar Regions
- ⮑ United States
  - ⮑ General
  - ⮑ African American
  - ⮑ Asian American
  - ⮑ Hispanic & Latino
  - ⮑ Native American
  - ⮑ Other

Performing Arts
- ⮑ General
- ⮑ Circus
- ⮑ Dance
- ⮑ Film
- ⮑ Music
- ⮑ Television & Radio
- ⮑ Theater

Politics & Government

Readers

Beginner

Chapter Books

Intermediate

Religious
- ⮑ General
- ⮑ Christian
  - ⮑ General
  - ⮑ Action & Adventure
  - ⮑ Animals

- ⮑ Bedtime & Dreams
- ⮑ Comics & Graphic Novels
- ⮑ Early Readers
- ⮑ Emotions & Feelings
- ⮑ Family
- ⮑ Fantasy
- ⮑ Friendship
- ⮑ Health & Daily Living
- ⮑ Historical
- ⮑ Holidays & Celebrations
- ⮑ Humorous
- ⮑ Learning Concepts
- ⮑ Mysteries & Detective Stories
- ⮑ People & Places
- ⮑ Relationships
- ⮑ Science Fiction
- ⮑ Social Issues
- ⮑ Sport & recreation
- ⮑ Values & Virtues
- ⮑ Jewish
- ⮑ Other

Robots

Royalty

School & Education

Science & Technology

Science Fiction

Short Stories

Social Issues
- ⮑ General
- ⮑ Adolescence
- ⮑ Bullying
- ⮑ Dating & Sex
- ⮑ Death & Dying
- ⮑ Depression & Mental Illness
- ⮑ Drugs, Alcohol, Substance Abuse
- ⮑ Emigrations & Immigration
- ⮑ Emotions & Feelings
- ⮑ Friendship
- ⮑ Homelessness & Poverty
- ⮑ Homosexuality
- ⮑ Manners & Etiquette
- ⮑ New Experience

- ➲ Peer Pressure
- ➲ Physical & Emotional Abuse
- ➲ Pregnancy
- ➲ Prejudice & Racism
- ➲ Runaways
- ➲ Self-Esteem & Self-Reliance
- ➲ Self Mutilation
- ➲ Sexual Abuse
- ➲ Special Needs
- ➲ Strangers
- ➲ Suicide
- ➲ Values & Virtues
- ➲ Violence

Sports & Recreation
- ➲ General
- ➲ Baseball & Softball
- ➲ Basketball
- ➲ Camping & Outdoor Activities
- ➲ Cycling
- ➲ Equestrian
- ➲ Extreme Sports
- ➲ Football
- ➲ Games
- ➲ Golf
- ➲ Hockey
- ➲ Ice Skating
- ➲ Martial Arts
- ➲ Miscellaneous
- ➲ Roller & In-Line Skating
- ➲ Skateboarding
- ➲ Soccer
- ➲ Water Sports
- ➲ Winter Sports
- ➲ Wrestling

Steampunk
Stories in Verse
Toys, Dolls, Puppets
Transportation
- ➲ General
- ➲ Aviation
- ➲ Boats, Ships & Underwater Craft
- ➲ Cars & Trucks
- ➲ Motorcycles
- ➲ Railroads & Trains

Visionary & Metaphysical
Westerns

Appendix C
Categories - Non Fiction

Antiques & Collectibles
- General
- Americana
- Art
- Autographs
- Books
- Bottles
- Buttons & Pins
- Canadiana
- Care & Restoration
- Clocks & Watches
- Coins, Currency & Medals
- Comics
- Dolls
- Figurines
- Firearms & Weapons
- Furniture
- Glass & Glassware
- Jewelry
- Kitchenware
- Magazines & Newspapers
- Military
- Non-Sports Cards
- Paper Ephemera
- Performing Arts
- Political
- Popular Culture
- Porcelain & China
- Postcards
- Posters
- Pottery & Ceramics
- Radios & Televisions
- Records
- Reference
- Rugs
- Silver, Gold & Other Metals
- Sports
- Sports Cards
  - General
  - Baseball
  - Basketball
  - Football
  - Hockey
- Stamps
- Teddy Bears
- Textiles & Costume
- Tobacco-Related
- Toy Animals
- Toys
- Transportation
- Wine

Architecture
- General
- Adaptive Reuse & renovation
- Annuals
- Buildings
  - General
  - Landmarks & Monuments
  - Public, Commercial & Industrial
  - Religious
  - Residential
- Codes & Standards
- Criticism
- Decoration & Ornament
- Design, Drafting, Drawing & Presentation
- Historic Preservation
  - General
  - Restoration Techniques
- History

- General
- Ancient & Classical
- Baroque & Rococo
- Contemporary
- Medieval
- Modern
- Prehistoric & Primitive
- Renaissance
- Romanticism
- Individual Architects & Firms
  - General
  - Essays
  - Monographs
- Interior Design
  - General
  - Lighting
- Landscape
- Methods & Materials
- Professional Practice
- Project Management
- Reference
- Regional
- Security Design
- Study & Teaching
- Sustainability & Green Design
- Urban & Land Use Planning

Art
- General
- African
- American
  - General
  - African American
  - Asian American
  - Hispanic American
- Annuals
- Art & Politics
- Asian
- Australian & Oceanian
- Body Art & tattooing
- Business Aspects
- Canadian

- Caribbean & Latin American
- Ceramics
- Collections, Catalogs, Exhibitions
  - General
  - Group Shows
  - Permanent Collections
- Color Theory
- Conceptual
- Conservation & Preservation
- Criticism & Theory
- Digital
- European
- Film & Video
- Folk & Outsider Art
- Graffiti & Street Art
- History
  - General
  - Ancient & Classical
  - Baroque & Rococo
  - Contemporary
  - Medieval
  - Modern
  - Prehistoric & Primitive
  - Renaissance
  - Romanticism
- Individual Artists
  - General
  - Artists' Books
  - Essays
  - Monographs
- Middle Eastern
- Mixed Media
- Museum Studies
- Native American
- Performance
- Popular Culture
- Prints
- Reference
- Russian & Former Soviet Union
- Sculpture & Installation
- Study & Teaching
- Subjects & Themes

- General
- Erotica
- Human Figure
- Landscapes & Seascapes
  - Plants & Animals
  - Portraits
  - Religious
- Techniques
  - General
  - Acrylic Painting
  - Airbrush
  - Calligraphy
  - Cartooning
  - Color
  - Drawing
  - Life Drawing
  - Oil Painting
  - Painting
  - Pastel Drawing
  - Pen & Ink Drawing
  - Pencil Drawing
  - Printmaking
  - Sculpting
  - Watercolor Painting

Bibles
- General
- Christian Standard Bible
  - General
  - Children
  - Devotional
  - New Testament & Portions
  - Reference
  - Study
  - Text
  - Youth & Teen
- Common English Bible
  - General
  - Children
  - Devotional
  - New Testament & Portions
  - Reference

- Study
- Text
- Youth & Teen
- Contemporary English Version
  - General
  - Children
  - Devotional
  - New Testament & Portions
  - Reference
  - Study
  - Text
  - Youth & Teen
- English Standard Version
  - General
  - Children
  - Devotional
  - New Testament & Portions
  - Reference
  - Study
  - Text
  - Youth & Teen
- God's Word
  - General
  - Children
  - Devotional
  - New Testament & Portions
  - Reference
  - Study
  - Text
  - Youth & Teen
- International Children's Bible
  - General
  - Children
  - Devotional
  - New Testament & Portions
  - Reference
  - Study
  - Text
  - Youth & Teen
- King James Version

- General
- Children
- Devotional
- New Testament & Portions
- Reference
- Study
- Text
- Youth & Teen
- Bad Biblia de las Americas
  - General
  - Children
  - Devotional
  - New Testament & Portions
  - Reference
  - Study
  - Text
  - Youth & Teen
- Multiple Translations
  - General
  - Children
  - Devotional
  - New Testament & Portions
  - Reference
  - Study
  - Text
  - Youth & Teen
- New American Bible
  - General
  - Children
  - Devotional
  - New Testament & Portions
  - Reference
  - Study
  - Text
  - Youth & Teen
- New American Standard Bible
  - General
  - Children
  - Devotional
  - New Testament & Portions

- Reference
- Study
- Text
- Youth & Teen
- New Century Version
  - General
  - Children
  - Devotional
  - New Testament & Portions
  - Reference
  - Study
  - Text
  - Youth & Teen
- New International Reader's Version
  - General
  - Children
  - Devotional
  - New Testament & Portions
  - Reference
  - Study
  - Text
  - Youth & Teen
- New International Version
  - General
  - Children
  - Devotional
  - New Testament & Portions
  - Reference
  - Study
  - Text
  - Youth & Teen
- New Kind James Version
  - General
  - Children
  - Devotional
  - New Testament & Portions
  - Reference
  - Study
  - Text
  - Youth & Teen
- New Living Translation

- General
- Children
- Devotional
- New Testament & Portions
- Reference
- Study
- Text
- Youth & Teen
- New Revised Standard Version
  - General
  - Children
  - Devotional
  - New Testament & Portions
  - Reference
  - Study
  - Text
  - Youth & Teen
- Nueva Version international
  - General
  - Children
  - Devotional
  - New Testament & Portions
  - Reference
  - Study
  - Text
  - Youth & Teen
- Other Translations
  - General
  - Children
  - Devotional
  - New Testament & Portions
  - Reference
  - Study
  - Text
  - Youth & Teen
- Reina Valera
  - General
  - Children
  - Devotional
  - New Testament & Portions

- Reference
- Study
- Text
- Youth & Teen
- The Message
  - General
  - Children
  - Devotional
  - New Testament & Portions
  - Reference
  - Study
  - Text
  - Youth & Teen
- Today's New International Version
  - General
  - Children
  - Devotional
  - New Testament & Portions
  - Reference
  - Study
  - Text
  - Youth & Teen

Biography & Autobiography
- General
- Adventurers & Explorers
- Artists, Architects, Photographers
- Business
- Composers & Musicians
- Criminals & Outlaws
- Culinary
- Cultural Heritage
- Editors, Journalists, Publishers
- Educators
- Entertainment & Performing Arts
- Environmentalists & Naturalists
- Historical
- Law Enforcement

- Lawyers & judges
- LGBT
- Literary
- Medical
- Military
- Native Americans
- People with Disabilities
- Personal Memoirs
- Philosophers
- Political
- Presidents & Heads of State
- Reference
- Religious
- Rich & Famous
- Royalty
- Science & Technology
- Social Activists
- Social Scientists & Psychologists
- Sports
- Women

Body, Mind & Spirit
- General
- Afterlife & Reincarnation
- Ancient Mysteries & Controversial Knowledge
- Angels & Spirit Guides
- Astrology
  - General
  - Eastern
  - Horoscopes
- Channeling & Mediumship
- Crystals
- Divination
  - General
  - Fortune Telling
  - Palmistry
  - Tarot
- Dreams
- Entheogens & Visionary Substances
- Feng Shui
- Gaia & Earth Energies
- Healing
  - General

- Energy
- Prayer & Spiritual
- Hermetism & Rosicrucianism
- I Ching
- Inspiration & Personal Growth
- Magick Studies
- Mysticism
- New Thought
- Numerology
- Occultism
- Parapsychology
  - General
  - ESP
  - Near-Death Experience
  - Out-of-Body Experience
- Prophecy
- Reference
- Sacred Sexuality
- Shamanism
- Spiritualism
- Spirituality
  - Celtic Spirituality
- Supernatural
- UFOs & Extraterrestrials
- Unexplained Phenomena
- Witchcraft

Business & Economics
- General
- Accounting
  - General
  - Financial
  - Governmental
  - Managerial
  - Standards
- Advertising & Promotion
- Auditing
- Banks & Banking
- Bookkeeping
- Budgeting
- Business Communication
  - General

⮂ Meetings & Presentations
⮂ Business Ethics
⮂ Business Etiquette
⮂ Business Law
⮂ Business Mathematics
⮂ Business Writing
⮂ Careers
  ⮂ General
  ⮂ Internships
  ⮂ Job Hunting
  ⮂ Resumes
⮂ Commerce
⮂ Commercial Policy
⮂ Conflict Resolution & Mediation
⮂ Consulting
⮂ Consumer Behavior
⮂ Corporate & Business History
⮂ Corporate Finance
  ⮂ General
  ⮂ Valuation
⮂ Corporate Governance
⮂ Crowdfunding
⮂ Customer Relations
⮂ Decision Making & Problem Solving
⮂ Development
  ⮂ General
  ⮂ Business Development
  ⮂ Economic Development
  ⮂ Sustainable Development
⮂ Distribution
⮂ E-Commerce
  ⮂ General
  ⮂ Auctions & Small Business
  ⮂ Internet Marketing
  ⮂ Online Trading
⮂ Econometrics
⮂ Economic Conditions
⮂ Economic History
⮂ Economics

⮂ General
⮂ Comparative
⮂ Macroeconomics
⮂ Microeconomics
⮂ Theory
⮂ Education
⮂ Entrepreneurship
⮂ Environmental Economics
⮂ Exports & Imports
⮂ Facility Management
⮂ Finance
  ⮂ General
⮂ Forcasting
⮂ Foreign Exchange
⮂ Franchises
⮂ Free Enterprise
⮂ Government & Business
⮂ Green Business
⮂ Home-Based Businesses
⮂ Human Resources & Personnel Management
⮂ Industrial Management
⮂ Industries
  ⮂ General
  ⮂ Agribusiness
  ⮂ Automobile Industry
  ⮂ Computers & Information Technology
  ⮂ Energy
  ⮂ Entertainment
  ⮂ Fashion & Textile
  ⮂ Industry
  ⮂ Financial Services
  ⮂ Food Industry
  ⮂ Hospitality, Travel & Tourism
  ⮂ Manufacturing
  ⮂ Media & Communications
  ⮂ Natural Resource Extraction
  ⮂ Park & Recreation Management
  ⮂ Pharmaceutical & Biotechnology
  ⮂ Retailing

- Service
- Transportation
- Inflation
- Information Management
- Infrastructure
- Insurance
  - General
  - Automobile
  - Casualty
  - Health
  - Liability
  - Life
  - Property
  - Risk Assessment & Management
- Interest
- International
  - General
  - Accounting
  - Economics
  - Marketing
  - Taxation
- Investments & Securities
  - General
  - Analysis & Trading Strategies
  - Bonds
  - Commodities
    - General
    - Energy
    - Metals
  - Derivatives
  - Futures
  - Mutual Funds
  - Options
  - Real Estate
  - Stocks
- Knowledge Capital
- Labor
- Leadership
- Mail Order
- Management
- Management Science
- Marketing
  - General
  - Direct

- Industrial
- Multilevel
- Research
- Telemarketing
- Mentoring & Coaching
- Mergers & Acquisitions
- Money & Monetary Policy
- Motivational
- Museum Administration & Museology
- Negotiating
- New Business Enterprises
- Nonprofit Organizations & Charities
  - General
  - Fundraising & Grants
  - Management & Leadership
  - Marketing & Communication
- Office Automation
- Office Equipment & Supplies
- Office Management
- Operations Research
- Organizational Behavior
- Organizational Development
- Outsourcing
- Personal Finance
  - General
  - Budgeting
  - Investing
  - Money Management
  - Retirement Planning
  - Taxation
- Personal Success
- Production & Operations Management
- Project Management
- Public Finance
- Public Relations
- Purchasing & Buying
- Quality Control
- Real Estate
  - General

- ➲ Buying & Selling
Homes
  - ➲ Commercial
  - ➲ Mortgages
- ➲ Reference
- ➲ Research & Development
- ➲ Sales & Selling
  - ➲ General
  - ➲ Management
- ➲ Secretarial Aids & Training
- ➲ Skills
- ➲ Small Business
- ➲ Statistics
- ➲ Strategic Planning
- ➲ Structural Adjustment
- ➲ Taxation
  - ➲ General
  - ➲ Corporate
  - ➲ Small Business
- ➲ Time Management
- ➲ Total Quality Management
- ➲ Training
- ➲ Urban & Regional
- ➲ Woman in Business
- ➲ Workplace Culture

Comics & Graphic Novels
- ➲ General
- ➲ Adaptations
- ➲ Anthologies
- ➲ Contemporary Women
- ➲ Crime & Mystery
- ➲ Erotica
- ➲ Fantasy
- ➲ Historical Fiction
- ➲ Horror
- ➲ LGBT
- ➲ Literary
- ➲ Manga
  - ➲ General
  - ➲ Adult Comics
  - ➲ Boys' Love Comics
  - ➲ Crime & Mystery
  - ➲ Erotica
  - ➲ Fantasy

- ➲ Historical Fiction
- ➲ Horror
- ➲ Illustrations & Fanbooks
- ➲ Josei Manga
- ➲ LGBT
- ➲ Media Tie-In
- ➲ Nonfiction
- ➲ Romance
- ➲ Science Fiction
- ➲ Seinen Manga
- ➲ Shonen Manga
- ➲ Shoujo Manga
- ➲ Sports
- ➲ Yaoi Manga
- ➲ Media Tie-In
- ➲ Nonfiction
- ➲ Religious
- ➲ Romance
- ➲ Science Fiction
- ➲ Superheroes

Computers
- ➲ General
- ➲ Bioinformatics
- ➲ Buyer's Guides
- ➲ CAD-CAM
- ➲ Calculators
- ➲ CD-DVD Technology
- ➲ Certification Guides
  - ➲ General
  - ➲ A+
  - ➲ MCSE
- ➲ Client-Server Computing
- ➲ Compilers
- ➲ Computer Engineering
- ➲ Computer Graphics
- ➲ Computer Literacy
- ➲ Computer Science
- ➲ Computer Simulation
- ➲ Computer Vision & Pattern Recognition
- ➲ Computerized Home & Entertainment
- ➲ Cybernetics

- ⊃ Data Modeling & Design
- ⊃ Data Processing
- ⊃ Data Transmission Systems
  - ⊃ General
  - ⊃ Broadband
  - ⊃ Electronic Data Interchange
  - ⊃ Wireless
- ⊃ Data Visualization
- ⊃ Databases
  - ⊃ General
  - ⊃ Data Mining
  - ⊃ Data Warehousing
  - ⊃ Servers
- ⊃ Desktop Applications
  - ⊃ General
  - ⊃ Databases
  - ⊃ Design & Graphics
  - ⊃ Desktop Publishing
  - ⊃ Email Clients
  - ⊃ Personal Finance Applications
  - ⊃ Presentation Software
  - ⊃ Project Management Software
  - ⊃ Spreadsheets
  - ⊃ Suites
  - ⊃ Word Processing
- ⊃ Digital Media
  - ⊃ General
  - ⊃ Audio
  - ⊃ Photography
  - ⊃ Video & Animation
- ⊃ Document Management
- ⊃ Documentation & Technical Writing
- ⊃ Educational Software
- ⊃ Electronic Commerce
- ⊃ Electronic Publishing
- ⊃ Enterprise Applications
  - ⊃ General
  - ⊃ Business Intelligence Tools
  - ⊃ Collaboration Software
- ⊃ Expert Systems
- ⊃ Hardware

- ⊃ General
- ⊃ Mainframes & Minicomputers
- ⊃ Mobile Devices
- ⊃ Peripherals
- ⊃ Personal Computers
  - ⊃ General
  - ⊃ Macintosh
  - ⊃ PCs
- ⊃ Tablets
- ⊃ History
- ⊃ Image Processing
- ⊃ Information Technology
- ⊃ Information Theory
- ⊃ Intelligence (AI) & Semantics
- ⊃ Interactive & Multimedia
- ⊃ Internet
  - ⊃ General
  - ⊃ Application Development
- ⊃ Keyboarding
- ⊃ Logic Design
- ⊃ Machine Theory
- ⊃ Management Information Systems
- ⊃ Mathematical & Statistical Software
- ⊃ Microprocessors
- ⊃ Natural Language Processing
- ⊃ Networking
  - ⊃ General
  - ⊃ Hardware
  - ⊃ Intranets & Extranets
  - ⊃ Local Area Networks
  - ⊃ Network Protocols
  - ⊃ Vendor Specific
- ⊃ Neural Networks
- ⊃ Online Services
- ⊃ Operating Systems
  - ⊃ General
  - ⊃ DOS
  - ⊃ Linux
  - ⊃ Macintosh
  - ⊃ Mainframe & Midrange

- UNIX
- Virtualization
- Windows Desktop
- Windows Server
- Optical Data Processing
- Programming
  - General
  - Algorithms
  - Games
  - Macintosh
  - Microsoft
  - Mobile Devices
  - Object Oriented
  - Open Source
  - Parallel
- Programming Languages
  - General
  - Ada
  - ASP.NET
  - Assembly Language
  - BASIC
  - C
  - C#
  - C++
  - COBOL
  - FORTRAN
  - HTML
  - Java
  - JavaScript
  - LISP
  - Pascal
  - Perl
  - PHP
  - Prolog
  - Python
  - RPG
  - Ruby
  - SQL
  - UML
  - VBScript
  - Visual BASIC
  - XML
- Reference
- Security
  - General
  - Cryptography

- Networking
- Online Safety & Privacy
  - Viruses & Malware
- Social Aspects
  - General
  - Human-Computer Interaction
- Software Development & Engineering
  - General
  - Project Management
  - Quality Assurance & Testing
  - Systems Analysis & Design
  - Tools
- Speech & Audio Processing
- System Administration
  - General
  - Disaster & Recovery
  - Email Administration
  - Storage & Retrieval
  - Windows Administration
- Systems Architecture
  - General
  - Distributed Systems & Computing
- User Interfaces
- Utilities
- Virtual Worlds
- Web
  - General
  - Blogs
  - Browsers
  - Content Management Systems
  - Design
  - Podcasting & Webcasting
  - Search Engines
  - Site Directories
  - Social Networking
  - User Generated Content

⮑ Web Programming
⮑ Web Services & APIs

Cooking
⮑ General
⮑ Baby Food
⮑ Beverages
   ⮑ General
   ⮑ Bartending
   ⮑ Beer
   ⮑ Coffee & Tea
   ⮑ Non-Alcoholic
   ⮑ Wine & Spirits
⮑ Courses & Dishes
   ⮑ General
   ⮑ Appetizers
   ⮑ Bread
   ⮑ Breakfast
   ⮑ Brunch
   ⮑ Cakes
   ⮑ Casseroles
   ⮑ Chocolate
   ⮑ Confectionery
   ⮑ Cookies
   ⮑ Desserts
   ⮑ Pastry
   ⮑ Pies
   ⮑ Salads
   ⮑ Sauces & Dressings
   ⮑ Soups & Stews
⮑ Entertaining
⮑ Essays & Narratives
⮑ Health & Healing
   ⮑ General
   ⮑ Allergy
   ⮑ Cancer
   ⮑ Diabetic & Sugar-Free
   ⮑ Gluten-Free
   ⮑ Heart
   ⮑ Low Carbohydrate
   ⮑ Low Cholesterol
   ⮑ Low Fat
   ⮑ Low Salt
   ⮑ Weight Control
⮑ History

⮑ Holiday
⮑ Methods
   ⮑ General
   ⮑ Baking
   ⮑ Barbecue & Grilling
   ⮑ Canning & Preserving
   ⮑ Cookery for One
   ⮑ Frying
   ⮑ Gourmet
   ⮑ Low Budget
   ⮑ Microwave
   ⮑ Outdoor
   ⮑ Professional
   ⮑ Quantity
   ⮑ Quick & Easy
   ⮑ Raw Food
   ⮑ Slow Cooking
   ⮑ Special Appliances
   ⮑ Wok
⮑ Reference
⮑ Regional & Ethnic
   ⮑ General
   ⮑ African
   ⮑ American
      ⮑ General
      ⮑ California Style
      ⮑ Middle Atlantic States
      ⮑ Middle Western States
      ⮑ New England
      ⮑ Northwestern States
      ⮑ Southern States
      ⮑ Southwestern States
      ⮑ Western States
   ⮑ Asian
   ⮑ Cajun & Creole
   ⮑ Canadian
   ⮑ Caribbean & West Indian
   ⮑ Central American & South American
   ⮑ Chinese

- ➲ English, Scottish & Welsh
  - ➲ European
  - ➲ French
  - ➲ German
  - ➲ Greek
  - ➲ Hungarian
  - ➲ Indian & South Asian
  - ➲ International
  - ➲ Irish
  - ➲ Italian
  - ➲ Japanese
  - ➲ Jewish & Kosher
  - ➲ Mediterranean
  - ➲ Mexican
  - ➲ Middle Eastern
  - ➲ Native American
  - ➲ Pacific Rim
  - ➲ Polish
  - ➲ Portuguese
  - ➲ Russian
  - ➲ Scandinavian
  - ➲ Soul Food
  - ➲ Spanish
  - ➲ Thai
  - ➲ Turkish
  - ➲ Vietnamese
- ➲ Seasonal
- ➲ Specific Ingredients
- ➲ Tablesetting
- ➲ Vegetarian & Vegan

Crafts & Hobbies
- ➲ General
- ➲ Applique
- ➲ Baskets
- ➲ Beadwork
- ➲ Book Printing & Binding
- ➲ Candle & Soup Making
- ➲ Carving
- ➲ Crafts for Children
- ➲ Decorating
- ➲ Dollhouses
- ➲ Dolls & Doll Clothing
- ➲ Dough

- ➲ Dye
- ➲ Fashion
- ➲ Flower Arranging
- ➲ Folkcrafts
- ➲ Framing
- ➲ Glass & Glassware
- ➲ Jewelry
- ➲ Knots, Macrame & Rope Work
- ➲ Leatherwork
- ➲ Metal Work
- ➲ Miniatures
- ➲ Mixed Media
- ➲ Model Railroading
- ➲ Models
- ➲ Nature Crafts
- ➲ Needlework
  - ➲ General
  - ➲ Crocheting
  - ➲ Cross-Stitch
  - ➲ embroidery
  - ➲ Knitting
  - ➲ Lace & Tatting
  - ➲ Needlepoint
- ➲ Origami
- ➲ Painting
- ➲ Papercrafts
- ➲ Patchwork
- ➲ Polymer Clay
- ➲ Potpourri
- ➲ Pottery & Ceramics
- ➲ Printmaking
- ➲ Puppets & Puppetry
- ➲ Quilts & Quilting
- ➲ Reference
- ➲ Rugs
- ➲ Scrapbooking
- ➲ Seasonal
- ➲ Sewing
- ➲ Stenciling
- ➲ Stuffed Animals
- ➲ Toymaking
- ➲ Weaving
- ➲ Wirework
- ➲ Wood Toys
- ➲ Woodwork

Design
- General
- Book
- Clip art
- Decorative Arts
- Essays
- Fashion
- Furniture
- Graphic Arts
  - General
  - Advertising
  - Branding & Logo Design
  - Commercial & Corporate
  - Illustration
  - Typography
- History & Criticism
- Industrial
- Interior Decorating
- Product
- Reference
- Textile & Costume

Drama
- General
- African
- American
  - General
  - African American
- Ancient & Classical
- Anthologies
- Asian
  - General
  - Japanese
- Australian & Oceanian
- Canadian
- Caribbean & Latin American
- European
  - General
  - English, Irish, Scottish, Welsh
    - French
    - German
    - Italian
    - Spanish & Portuguese
- LGBT
- Medieval
- Middle Eastern
- Religious & Liturgical
- Russian & Former Soviet Union
- Shakespeare
- Women Authors

Education
- General
- Administration
  - General
  - Elementary & Secondary
    - Facility Management
    - Higher
    - School Superintendents & Principals
- Adult & Continuing Education
- Aims & Objectives
- Arts in Education
- Behavioral Management
- Bilingual Education
- Classroom Management
- Collaborative & Team Teaching
- Comparative
- Computers & Technology
- Counseling
  - General
  - Academic Development
    - Crisis Management
- Curricula
- Decision-Making & Problem Solving
- Distance & Online Education

- ⊃ Driver Education
- ⊃ Educational Policy & Reform
  - ⊃ General
  - ⊃ Charter Schools
  - ⊃ Federal Legislation
  - ⊃ School Safety
- ⊃ Educational Psychology
- ⊃ Elementary
- ⊃ Essays
- ⊃ Evaluation & Assessment
- ⊃ Experimental Methods
- ⊃ Finance
- ⊃ Higher
- ⊃ History
- ⊃ Home Schooling
- ⊃ Inclusive Education
- ⊃ Language Experience Approach
- ⊃ Leadership
- ⊃ Learning Styles
- ⊃ Multicultural Education
- ⊃ Non-Formal Education
- ⊃ Organizations & institutions
- ⊃ Parent Participation
- ⊃ Philosophy & Social Aspects
- ⊃ Physical Education
- ⊃ Preschool & Kindergarten
- ⊃ Professional Development
- ⊃ Reference
- ⊃ Research
- ⊃ Rural
- ⊃ Secondary
- ⊃ Special Education
  - ⊃ General
  - ⊃ Communicative Disorders
  - ⊃ Gifted
  - ⊃ Learning Disabilities
  - ⊃ Mental Disabilities
  - ⊃ Physical Disabilities
  - ⊃ Social Disabilities
- ⊃ Statistics
- ⊃ Student Life & Student Affairs

- ⊃ Study Skills
- ⊃ Teaching Methods & Materials
  - ⊃ General
  - ⊃ Arts & Humanities
  - ⊃ Health & Sexuality
  - ⊃ Language Arts
  - ⊃ Library Skills
  - ⊃ Mathematics
  - ⊃ Reading & Phonics
  - ⊃ Science & Technology
  - ⊃ Social Science
- ⊃ Testing & Measurement
- ⊃ Training & Certification
- ⊃ Urban
- ⊃ Violence & Harassment
- ⊃ Vocational

Family & Relationships
- ⊃ General
- ⊃ Abuse
  - ⊃ General
  - ⊃ Child Abuse
  - ⊃ Domestic Partner Abuse
  - ⊃ Elder Abuse
- ⊃ Activities
- ⊃ Adoption & Fostering
- ⊃ Alternative Family
- ⊃ Anger
- ⊃ Attention Deficit Disorder
- ⊃ Autism Spectrum Disorders
- ⊃ Baby Names
- ⊃ Babysitting, Day Care & Child Care
- ⊃ Bullying
- ⊃ Children with Special Needs
- ⊃ Conflict Resolution
- ⊃ Dating
- ⊃ Death, Grief, Bereavement
- ⊃ Divorce & Separation
- ⊃ Dysfunctional Families
- ⊃ Education
- ⊃ Eldercare

- Extended Family
- Friendship
- Learning Disabilities
- Life Stages
  - General
  - Adolescence
  - Infants & Toddlers
  - School Age
  - Teenagers
- Love & Romance
- Marriage & Long Term Relationships
- Military Families
- Parenting
  - General
  - Fatherhood
  - Grandparenting
  - Motherhood
  - Parent & Adult Child
  - Single Parent
  - Stepparenting
- Peer Pressure
- Prejudice
- Reference
- Siblings
- Toilet Training

Foreign Language Study
- General
- African Languages
- Ancient Languages
- Arabic
- Baltic Languages
- Celtic Languages
- Chinese
- Creole Languages
- Czech
- Danish
- Dutch
- English as a Second Language
- Finnish
- French
- German
- Greek

- Hebrew
- Hindi
- Hungarian
- Indic Languages
- Italian
- Japanese
- Korean
- Latin
- Miscellaneous
- Multi-Language Dictionaries
- Multi-Language Phrasebooks
- Native American Languages
- Norwegian
- Oceanic & Australian Languages
- Old & Middle English
- Persian
- Polish
- Portuguese
- Romance Languages
- Russian
- Scandinavian Languages
- Serbian & Croatian
- Slavic Languages
- Southeast Asian Languages
- Spanish
- Swahili
- Swedish
- Turkish & Turkic Languages
- Vietnamese
- Yiddish

Games
- General
- Backgammon
- Board
- Card Games
  - General
  - Blackjack
  - Bridge
  - Poker
  - Solitaire

- Checkers
- Chess
- Crosswords
  - General
  - Dictionaries
- Fantasy Sports
- Gambling
  - General
  - Lotteries
  - Sports
  - Table
  - Track Betting
- Logic & Brain Teasers
- Magic
- Optical Illusions
- Puzzles
- Quizzes
- Reference
- Role Playing & Fantasy
- Sudoku
- Travel Games
- Trivia
- Video & Electronic
- Word & Word Search

Gardening
- General
- Climatic
  - General
  - Desert
  - Temperate
  - Tropical
- Container
- Essays & Narratives
- Flowers
  - General
  - Annuals
  - Bulbs
  - Orchids
  - Perennials
  - Roses
  - Wildflowers
- Fruit
- Garden Design
- Garden Furnishing

- Greenhouses
- Herbs
- House Plants & Indoor
- Japanese Gardens
- Landscape
- Lawns
- Organic
- Ornamental Plants
- Reference
- Regional
  - General
  - Canada
  - Middle Atlantic
  - Midwest
  - New England
  - Pacific Northwest
  - South
  - Southwest
  - West
- Shade
- Shrubs
- Techniques
- Topiary
- Trees
- Urban
- Vegetables

Health & Fitness
- General
- Acupressure & Acupuncture
- Aerobics
- Allergies
- Alternative Therapies
- Aromatherapy
- Beauty & Grooming
- Body Cleansing & Detoxification
- Breastfeeding
- Children's Health
- Diet & Nutrition
  - General
  - Diets
  - Food Content Guides
  - Macrobiotics
  - Nutrition
  - Vitamins

- ➲ Weight Loss
- ➲ Diseases
  - ➲ General
  - ➲ AIDS & HIV
  - ➲ Alzheimer's & Dementia
  - ➲ Cancer
  - ➲ Chronic Fatigue Syndrome
  - ➲ Contagious
  - ➲ Diabetes
  - ➲ Gastrointestinal
  - ➲ Genetic
  - ➲ Genitourinary & STDs
  - ➲ Heart
  - ➲ Musculoskeletal
  - ➲ Nervous System
  - ➲ Respiratory
  - ➲ Skin
- ➲ Endocrine System
- ➲ Exercise
- ➲ First Aid
- ➲ Healing
- ➲ Health Care Issues
- ➲ Healthy Living
- ➲ Hearing & Speech
- ➲ Herbal Medications
- ➲ Holism
- ➲ Infertility
- ➲ Massage & Reflexotherapy
- ➲ Men's Health
- ➲ Naturopathy
- ➲ Oral Health
- ➲ Pain Management
- ➲ Physical Impairments
- ➲ Pregnancy & Childbirth
- ➲ Reference
- ➲ Safety
- ➲ Sexuality
- ➲ Sleep & Sleep Disorders
- ➲ Vision
- ➲ Women's Health
- ➲ Work-Related Health
- ➲ Yoga

History
- ➲ General
- ➲ Africa
  - ➲ General
  - ➲ Central
  - ➲ East
  - ➲ North
  - ➲ South
    - ➲ General
    - ➲ Republic of South Africa
  - ➲ West
- ➲ Americas
- ➲ Ancient
  - ➲ General
  - ➲ Egypt
  - ➲ Greece
  - ➲ Rome
- ➲ Asia
  - ➲ General
  - ➲ Central Asia
  - ➲ China
  - ➲ India & South Asia
  - ➲ Japan
  - ➲ Korea
  - ➲ Southeast Asia
- ➲ Australia & New Zealand
- ➲ Canada
  - ➲ General
  - ➲ Post-Confederation
  - ➲ Pre-Confederation
- ➲ Caribbean & West Indies
  - ➲ General
  - ➲ Cuba
- ➲ Civilization
- ➲ Essays
- ➲ Europe
  - ➲ General
  - ➲ Austria & Hungary
  - ➲ Baltic States
  - ➲ Eastern
  - ➲ Former Soviet Republics
  - ➲ France
  - ➲ Germany
  - ➲ Great Britain

- Greece
- Ireland
- Italy
- Russia & the Former Soviet Union
- Scandinavia
- Spain & Portugal
- Western
- Expeditions & Discoveries
- Historical Geography
- Historiography
- Holocaust
- Jewish
- Latin America
  - General
  - Central America
  - Mexico
  - South America
- Medieval
- Middle East
  - General
  - Arabian Peninsula
  - Egypt
  - Iran
  - Iraq
  - Israel & Palestine
  - Turkey & Ottoman Empire
- Military
  - General
  - Afghan War
  - Aviation
  - Biological & Chemical Warfare
  - Canada
  - Iraq War
  - Korean War
  - Naval
  - Nuclear Warfare
  - Other
  - Persian Gulf War
  - Pictorial
  - Special Forces
  - Strategy
  - United States
  - Veterans

- Vietnam War
- Weapons
- World War I
- World War II
- Modern
  - General
  - 16th Century
  - 17th Century
  - 18th Century
  - 19th Century
  - 20th Century
  - 21st Century
- Native American
- North American
- Oceania
- Polar Regions
- Reference
- Renaissance
- Revolutionary
- Social History
- Study & Teaching
- United States
  - General
  - 19th Century
  - 20th Century
  - 21st Century
  - Civil War Period
  - Colonial Period
  - Revolutionary Period
  - State & Local
    - General
    - Middle Atlantic
    - Midwest
    - New England
    - Pacific Northwest
    - South
    - Southwest
    - West
- World

House & Home
- General
- Cleaning, Caretaking & Organizing
- Decorating

- Design & Construction
- Do-It-Yourself
  - General
  - Carpentry
  - Electrical
  - Masonry
  - Plumbing
- Equipment, Appliances & Supplies
- Furniture
- Hand Tools
- House Plans
- Outdoor & Recreational Areas
- Power Tools
- Reference
- Remodeling & Renovation
- Repair
- Security
- Sustainable Living
- Woodworking

Humor
- General
- Form
  - Anecdotes & Quotations
  - Comic Strips & Cartoons
  - Essays
  - Jokes & Riddles
  - Limericks & Verse
  - Parodies
  - Pictorial
  - Puns & Word Play
  - Trivia
- Topic
  - Adult
  - Animals
  - Business & Professional
  - Language
  - Marriage & Family
  - Political
  - Relationships

- Religion
- Sports

Juvenile Non Fiction
- General
- Activity Books
- Adventure & Adventurers
- Animals
  - General
  - Animal Welfare
  - Apes, Monkeys, etc.
  - Baby Animals
  - Bears
  - Birds
  - Butterflies, Moths & Caterpillars
  - Cats
  - Cows
  - Deer, Moose & Caribou
  - Dinosaurs & Prehistoric Creatures
  - Dogs
  - Ducks, Geese, etc.
  - Elephants
  - Endangered
  - Farm Animals
  - Fishes
  - Foxes
  - Giraffes
  - Hippos & Rhinos
  - Horses
  - Insects, Spiders, etc.
  - Jungle Animals
  - Kangaroos
  - Lions, Tigers, Leopards, etc.
  - Mammals
  - Marine Life
  - Mice, Hamsters, Guinea Pigs, Squirrels, etc.
  - Nocturnal
  - Pets
  - Rabbits
  - Reptiles & Amphibians
  - Wolves & Coyotes

- Zoos
- Antiques & Collectibles
- Architecture
- Art
  - General
  - Cartooning
  - Drawing
  - Fashion
  - History
  - Painting
  - Sculpture
  - Techniques
- Biography & Autobiography
  - General
  - Art
  - Cultural Heritage
  - Historical
  - Literary
  - Music
  - Performing Arts
  - Political
  - Presidents & First Families
  - Religious
  - Royalty
  - Science & Technology
  - Social Activists
  - Sports & Recreation
  - Women
- Body, Mind & Spirit
- Books & Libraries
- Boys & Men
- Business & Economics
- Careers
- Clothing & Dress
- Comics & Graphic Novels
  - General
  - Biography
  - History
- Computers
  - General
  - Entertainment & Games
  - Internet
  - Programming
  - Software

- Concepts
  - General
  - Alphabet
  - Body
  - Colors
  - Counting & Numbers
  - Date & Time
  - Money
  - Opposites
  - Seasons
  - Senses & Sensation
  - Size & Shape
  - Sounds
- Cooking & Food
- Crafts & Hobbies
- Curiosities & Wonders
- Drama
- Family
  - General
  - Adoption
  - Alternative Family
  - Marriage & Divorce
  - Multigenerational
  - New Baby
  - Orphans & Foster Homes
  - Parents
  - Siblings
  - Stepfamilies
- Foreign Language Study
  - General
  - English as a Second Language
  - French
  - Spanish
- Games & Activities
  - General
  - Board Games
  - Card Games
  - Magic
  - Puzzles
  - Questions & Answers
  - Video & Electronic Games
  - Word Games
- Gardening

- Girls & Women
- Health & Daily Living
  - General
  - Daily Activities
  - Diet & Nutrition
  - Diseases, Illnesses & Injuries
  - First Aid
  - Fitness & Exercise
  - Maturing
  - Personal Hygiene
  - Physical Impairments
  - Safety
  - Sexuality & Pregnancy
  - Substance Abuse
  - Toilet Training
- History
  - General
  - Africa
  - Ancient
  - Asia
  - Australia & Oceania
  - Canada
    - General
    - Post-Confederation
    - Pre-Confederation
  - Central & South America
  - Europe
  - Exploration & Discovery
  - Holocaust
  - Medieval
  - Mexico
  - Middle East
  - Military & Wars
  - Modern
  - Other
  - Prehistoric
  - Renaissance
  - Symbols, Monuments, National Parks, etc.
  - United States
    - General

- 19th Century
- 20th Century
- 21st Century
- Civil War Period
- Colonial & Revolutionary Periods
  - State & Local
- Holidays & Celebrations
  - General
  - Birthdays
  - Christmas & Advent
  - Easter & Lent
  - Halloween
  - Hanukkah
  - Kwanzaa
  - Other, Non-Religious
  - Other, Religious
  - Passover
  - Patriotic Holidays
  - Thanksgiving
  - Valentine's Day
- House & Home
- Humor
  - General
  - Comic Strips & Cartoons
  - Jokes & Riddles
- Language Arts
  - General
  - Composition & Creative Writing
  - Grammar
  - Handwriting
  - Sign Language
  - Vocabulary & Spelling
- Law & Crime
- Lifestyles
  - City & Town Life
  - Country Life
  - Farm & Ranch Life
- Literary Criticism & Collections
- Mathematics
  - General
  - Advanced
  - Algebra

- Arithmetic
- Fractions
- Geometry
- Media Studies
- Media Tie-In
- Music
  - General
  - Classical
  - History
  - Instruction & Study
  - Instruments
  - Jazz
  - Popular
  - Rap & Hip Hop
  - Rock
  - Songbooks
- People & Places
  - General
  - Africa
  - Asia
  - Australia & Oceania
  - Canada
    - General
    - Native Canadian
  - Caribbean & Latin America
  - Europe
  - Mexico
  - Middle East
  - Other
  - Polar Regions
  - United States
    - General
    - African American
    - Asian American
    - Hispanic & Latino
    - Native American
    - Other
- Performing Arts
  - General
  - Circus
  - Dance
  - Film
  - Television & Radio
  - Theater
- Philosophy

- Photography
- Poetry
  - General
  - Humorous
- Readers
  - Beginner
  - Chapter Books
  - Intermediate
- Recycling & Green Living
- Reference
  - General
  - Almanacs
  - Atlases
  - Dictionaries
  - Encyclopedias
  - Thesauri
- Religion
  - General
  - Bible Stories
    - General
    - New Testament
    - Old Testament
  - Biblical Biography
  - Biblical Commentaries & Interpretation
  - Biblical Reference
  - Biblical Studies
  - Christianity
  - Eastern
  - Islam
  - Judaism
- Religious
  - Christian
    - General
    - Biography & Autobiography
    - Comics & Graphic Novels
    - Devotional & Prayer
    - Early Readers
    - Family & Relationships
    - Games & Activities

➲ Health & Daily Living
➲ Holidays & Celebrations
➲ Inspirational
➲ Learning Concepts
➲ Science & Nature
➲ Social Issues
➲ Values & Virtues
➲ School & Education
➲ Science & Nature
  ➲ General
  ➲ Anatomy & Physiology
  ➲ Astronomy
  ➲ Biology
  ➲ Botany
  ➲ Chemistry
  ➲ Disasters
  ➲ Discoveries
  ➲ Earth Sciences
    ➲ General
    ➲ Earthquakes & Volcanoes
    ➲ Geography
    ➲ Rocks & Minerals
    ➲ Water
    ➲ Weather
  ➲ Environmental Conservation & Protection
  ➲ Environmental Science & Ecosystems
  ➲ Experiments & Projects
  ➲ Flowers & Plants
  ➲ Fossils
  ➲ History of Science
  ➲ Physics
  ➲ Trees & Forests
  ➲ Weights & Measures
  ➲ Zoology
➲ Social Issues
  ➲ General
  ➲ Adolescence
  ➲ Bullying
  ➲ Dating & Sex
  ➲ Death & Dying

➲ Depression & Mental Illness
➲ Drugs, Alcohol, Substance Abuse
➲ Emigration & Immigration
➲ Emotions & Feelings
➲ Friendship
➲ Homelessness & Poverty
➲ Homosexuality
➲ Manners & Etiquette
➲ New Experience
➲ Peer Pressure
➲ Physical & Emotional Abuse
➲ Pregnancy
➲ Prejudice & Racism
➲ Runaways
➲ Self-Esteem & Self-Reliance
➲ Self-Mutilation
➲ Sexual Abuse
➲ Special Needs
➲ Strangers
➲ Suicide
➲ Values & Virtues
➲ Violence
➲ Social Science
  ➲ General
  ➲ Archaeology
  ➲ Customs, Traditions, Anthropology
  ➲ Folklore & Mythology
  ➲ Politics & Government
  ➲ Psychology
  ➲ Sociology
➲ Sports & Recreation
  ➲ General
  ➲ Baseball & Softball
  ➲ Basketball
  ➲ Camping & Outdoor Activities
  ➲ Cycling
  ➲ Equestrian
  ➲ Extreme Sports

- Football
- Gold
- Gymnastics
- Hockey
- Ice Skating
- Martial Arts
- Miscellaneous
- Motor Sports
- Olympics
- Racket Sports
- Roller & In-Line Skating
- Skateboarding
- Soccer
- Track & Field
- Water Sports
- Winter Sports
- Wrestling
- Study Aids
  - General
  - Book Notes
  - Test Preparation
- Technology
  - General
  - Aeronautics, Astronautics & Space Science
  - Agriculture
  - Electricity & Electronics
  - How Things Work-Are Made
  - Inventions
  - Machinery & Tools
- Toys, Dolls & Puppets
- Transportation
  - General
  - Aviation
  - Boats, Ships & Underwater Craft
  - Cars & Trucks
  - Motorcycles
  - Railroads & Trains
- Travel

Language Arts & Disciplines

- General
- Alphabets & Writing Systems
- Authorship
- Communication Studies
- Composition & Creative Writing
- Editing & Proofreading
- Grammar & Punctuation
- Handwriting
- Journalism
- Lexicography
- Library & Information Science
  - General
  - Administration & Management
  - Archives & Special Libraries
  - Cataloging & Classification
  - Collection Development
  - Digital & Online Resources
  - School Media
- Linguistics
  - General
  - Etymology
  - Historical & Comparative
  - Morphology
  - Phonetics & Phonology
  - Pragmatics
  - Psycholinguistics
  - Semantics
  - Sociolinguistics
  - Syntax
- Literacy
- Public Speaking
- Publishing
- Readers
- Reading Skills
- Reference
- Rhetoric
- Sign Language

- Speech
- Spelling
- Study & Teaching
- Style Manuals
- Translating & Interpreting
- Vocabulary

Law
- General
- Administrative Law & Regulatory Practice
- Agricultural
- Air & Space
- Alternative Dispute Resolution
- Annotations & Citations
- Antitrust
- Arbitration, Negotiation, Mediation
- Banking
- Bankruptcy & Insolvency
- Business & Financial
- Child Advocacy
- Civil Law
- Civil Rights
- Commercial
  - General
  - International Trade
- Common
- Communications
- Comparative
- Computer & Internet
- Conflict of Laws
- Constitutional
- Construction
- Consumer
- Contracts
- Corporate
- Court Records
- Court Rules
- Courts
- Criminal Law
  - General
  - Juvenile Offenders
  - Sentencing

- Criminal Procedure
- Customary
- Defamation
- Depositions
- Dictionaries & Terminology
- Disability
- Discrimination
- Educational Law & Legislation
- Elder Law
- Election Law
- Emigration & Immigration
- Entertainment
- Environmental
- Essays
- Estates & Trusts
- Ethics & Professional Responsibility
- Evidence
- Family Law
  - General
  - Children
  - Divorce & Separation
  - Marriage
- Forensic Science
- Gender & the Law
- General Practice
- Government
  - General
  - Federal
  - State, Provincial & Municipal
- Health
- Housing & Urban Development
- Indigenous Peoples
- Insurance
- Intellectual Property
  - General
  - Copyright
  - Patent
  - Trademark
- International
- Judicial Power
- Jurisprudence
- Jury

- Labor & Employment
- Land Use
- Landlord & Tenant
- Law Office Management
- Legal Education
- Legal History
- Legal Profession
- Legal Services
- Legal Writing
- Liability
- Litigation
- Living Trusts
- Malpractice
- Maritime
- Media & the Law
- Medical Law & Legislation
- Mental Health
- Mergers & Acquisitions
- Military
- Natural Law
- Natural Resources
- Paralegals & Paralegalism
- Pension Law
- Personal Injury
- Practical Guides
- Privacy
- Property
- Public
- Public Contract
- Public Utilities
- Real Estate
- Reference
- Remedies & Damages
- Research
- Right to Die
- Science & Technology
- Securities
- Sports
- Taxation
- Torts
- Transportation
- Trial Practice
- Wills
- Witnesses

Literary Collections
- General
- African
- American
  - General
  - African American
- Ancient & Classical
- Asian
  - General
  - Chinese
  - Indic
  - Japanese
- Australian & Oceanian
- Canadian
- Caribbean & Latin American
- Diaries & Journals
- Essays
- European
  - General
  - Eastern
  - English, Irish, Scottish, Welsh
  - French
  - German
  - Italian
  - Scandinavian
  - Spanish & Portuguese
- Letters
- LGBT
- Medieval
- Middle Eastern
- Native American
- Russian & Former Soviet Union
- Speeches
- Women Authors

Literary Criticism
- General
- African
- American
  - General
  - African American
  - Asian American

- ➲ Hispanic American
- ➲ Ancient & Classical
- ➲ Asian
  - ➲ General
  - ➲ Chinese
  - ➲ Indic
  - ➲ Japanese
    - ➲ General
    - ➲ Japanese Literature
- ➲ Australian & Oceanian
- ➲ Books & Reading
- ➲ Canadian
- ➲ Caribbean & Latin American
- ➲ Children's Literature
- ➲ Comics & Graphic Novels
- ➲ Comparative Literature
- ➲ Drama
- ➲ European
  - ➲ General
  - ➲ Eastern
  - ➲ English, Irish, Scottish, Welsh
  - ➲ French
  - ➲ German
  - ➲ Italian
  - ➲ Scandinavian
  - ➲ Spanish & Portuguese
- ➲ Fairy Tales, Folk Tales, Legends & Mythology
- ➲ Feminist
- ➲ Gothic & Romance
- ➲ Horror & Supernatural
- ➲ Humor
- ➲ Jewish
- ➲ LGBT
- ➲ Medieval
- ➲ Middle Eastern
- ➲ Mystery & Detective
- ➲ Native American
- ➲ Poetry
- ➲ Reference
- ➲ Renaissance
- ➲ Russian & Former Soviet Union

- ➲ Science Fiction & Fantasy
- ➲ Semiotics & Theory
- ➲ Shakespeare
- ➲ Short Stories
- ➲ Women Authors

Mathematics
- ➲ General
- ➲ Algebra
  - ➲ General
  - ➲ Abstract
  - ➲ Elementary
  - ➲ Intermediate
  - ➲ Linear
- ➲ Applied
- ➲ Arithmetic
- ➲ Calculus
- ➲ Combinatorics
- ➲ Complex Analysis
- ➲ Counting & Numeration
- ➲ Differential Equations
  - ➲ General
  - ➲ Ordinary
  - ➲ Partial
- ➲ Discrete Mathematics
- ➲ Essays
- ➲ Finite Mathematics
- ➲ Functional Analysis
- ➲ Game Theory
- ➲ Geometry
  - ➲ General
  - ➲ Algebraic
  - ➲ Analytic
  - ➲ Differential
  - ➲ Non-Euclidean
- ➲ Graphic Methods
- ➲ Group Theory
- ➲ History & Philosophy
- ➲ Infinity
- ➲ Linear & Nonlinear Programming
- ➲ Logic
- ➲ Mathematical Analysis
- ➲ Matrices
- ➲ Measurement

- ⊃ Number Systems
- ⊃ Number Theory
- ⊃ Numerical Analysis
- ⊃ Optimization
- ⊃ Pre-Calculus
- ⊃ Probability & Statistics
    - ⊃ General
    - ⊃ Bayesian Analysis
    - ⊃ Multivariate Analysis
    - ⊃ Regression Analysis
    - ⊃ Stochastic Processes
    - ⊃ Time Series
- ⊃ Recreations & Games
- ⊃ Reference
- ⊃ Research
- ⊃ Set Theory
- ⊃ Study & Teaching
- ⊃ Topology
- ⊃ Transformations
- ⊃ Trigonometry
- ⊃ Vector Analysis

Medical
- ⊃ General
- ⊃ Acupuncture
- ⊃ Administration
- ⊃ AIDS & HIV
- ⊃ Allied Health Services
    - ⊃ General
    - ⊃ Emergency Medical Services
    - ⊃ Hypnotherapy
    - ⊃ Massage Therapy
    - ⊃ Medical Assistants
    - ⊃ Medical Technology
    - ⊃ Occupational Therapy
    - ⊃ Physical Therapy
    - ⊃ Radiological & Ultrasound Technology
- ⊃ Respiratory Therapy
- ⊃ Alternative & Complementary Medicine
- ⊃ Anatomy
- ⊃ Anesthesiology
- ⊃ Atlases

- ⊃ Audiology & Speech Pathology
- ⊃ Bariatrics
- ⊃ Biochemistry
- ⊃ Biostatistics
- ⊃ Biotechnology
- ⊃ Cardiology
- ⊃ Caregiving
- ⊃ Chemotherapy
- ⊃ Chiropractic
- ⊃ Clinical Medicine
- ⊃ Critical Care
- ⊃ Dentistry
    - ⊃ General
    - ⊃ Dental Assisting
    - ⊃ Dental Hygiene
    - ⊃ Dental Implants
    - ⊃ Endodontics
    - ⊃ Oral Surgery
    - ⊃ Orthodontics
    - ⊃ Periodontics
    - ⊃ Practice Management
    - ⊃ Prosthodontics
- ⊃ Dermatology
- ⊃ Diagnosis
- ⊃ Diagnostic Imaging
- ⊃ Dictionaries & Terminology
- ⊃ Diet Therapy
- ⊃ Diseases
- ⊃ Drug Guides
- ⊃ Education & Training
- ⊃ Embryology
- ⊃ Emergency Medicine
- ⊃ Endocrinology & Metabolism
- ⊃ Epidemiology
- ⊃ Essays
- ⊃ Ethics
- ⊃ Evidence-Based Medicine
- ⊃ Family & General Practice
- ⊃ Forensic Medicine
- ⊃ Gastroenterology
- ⊃ Genetics
- ⊃ Geriatrics
- ⊃ Gynecology & Obstetrics
- ⊃ Healing

- Health Care Delivery
- Health Policy
- Health Risk Assessment
- Hematology
- Hepatology
- Histology
- History
- Holistic Medicine
- Home Care
- Hospital Administration & Care
- Immunology
- Infection Control
- Infectious Diseases
- Instruments &Supplies
- Internal Medicine
- Laboratory Medicine
- Lasers in Medicine
- Long-Term Care
- Medicaid & Medicare
- Medical History & Records
- Mental Health
- Microbiology
- Nephrology
- Neurology
- Neuroscience
- Nosology
- Nursing
  - General
  - Anesthesia
  - Assessment & Diagnosis
  - Critical & Intensive Care
  - Emergency
  - Fundamentals & Skills
  - Gerontology
  - Home & Community Care
  - Issues
  - LPN & LVN
  - Management & Leadership
  - Maternity, Perinatal, Women's Health
  - Medical & Surgical

- Mental Health
- Nurse & Patient
- Nutrition
- Oncology & Cancer
- Pediatric & Neonatal
- Pharmacology
- Psychiatric
- Reference
- Research & Theory
- Test Preparation & Review
- Nursing Home Care
- Nutrition
- Occupational & Industrial Medicine
- Oncology
- Ophthalmology
- Optometry
- Orthopedics
- Osteopathy
- Otorhinolaryngology
- Pain Medicine
- Parasitology
- Pathology
- Pathophysiology
- Pediatrics
- Perinatology & Neonatology
- Pharmacology
- Pharmacy
- Physical Medicine & Rehabilitation
- Physician & Patient
- Physicians
- Physiology
- Podiatry
- Practice Management & Reimbursement
- Preventive Medicine
- Prosthesis
- Psychiatry
  - General
  - Child & Adolescent
  - Psychopharmacology
- Public Health
- Pulmonary & Thoracic Medicine

- Radiology & Nuclear Medicine
- Reference
- Reproductive Medicine & Technology
- Research
- Rheumatology
- Sports Medicine
- Surgery
    - General
    - Colon & Rectal
    - Neurosurgery
    - Oral & Maxillofacial
    - Plastic & Cosmetic
    - Thoracic
    - Transplant
    - Vascular
- Terminal Care
- Test Preparation & Review
- Toxicology
- Transportation
- Tropical Medicine
- Ultrasonography
- Urology
- Veterinary Medicine
    - General
    - Equine
    - Food Animal
    - Small Animal

Music
- General
- Business Aspects
- Discography & Buyer's Guides
- Ethnic
- Ethnomusicology
- Genres & Styles
    - General
    - Ballet
    - Big Band & Swing
    - Blues
    - Chamber
    - Children's
    - Choral

- Classical
- Country & Bluegrass
- Dance
- Electronic
- Folk & traditional
- Heavy Metal
- International
- Jazz
- Latin
- Military & Marches
- Musicals
- New Age
- Opera
- Pop Vocal
- Punk
- Rap & Hip Hop
- Reggae
- Rock
- Soul & R 'n B
- History & Criticism
- Individual Composer & Musician
- Instruction & Study
    - General
    - Appreciation
    - Composition
    - Conducting
    - Exercises
    - Songwriting
    - Techniques
    - Theory
    - Voice
- Lyrics
- Musical Instruments
    - General
    - Brass
    - Guitar
    - Percussion
    - Piano & Keyboard
    - Strings
    - Woodwinds
- Printed Music
    - General
    - Artist Specific
    - Band & Orchestra
    - Brass

- Choral
- Guitar & Fretted
Instruments
- Mixed Collections
- Musicals, Film & TV
- Opera & Classical
Scores
- Percussion
- Piano & Keyboard
Repertoire
- Piano-Vocal-Guitar
- Strings
- Vocal
- Woodwinds
- Recording & Reproduction
- Reference
- Religious
  - General
  - Christian
  - Contemporary
Christian
  - Gospel
  - Hymns
  - Jewish
  - Muslim

Nature
- General
- Animal Rights
- Animals
  - General
  - Bears
  - Big Cats
  - Birds
  - Butterflies & Moths
  - Dinosaurs & Prehistoric
Creatures
  - Fish
  - Horses
  - Insects & Spiders
  - Mammals
  - Marine Life
  - Primates
  - Reptiles & Amphibians
  - Wildlife

- Wolves
- Birdwatching Guides
- Earthquakes & Volcanoes
- Ecology
- Ecosystems & Habitats
  - General
  - Coastal Regions &
Shorelines
  - Deserts
  - Forests & Rainforests
  - Lakes, Ponds &
Swamps
  - Mountains
  - Oceans & Seas
  - Plains & Prairies
  - Polar Regions
  - Rivers
  - Wilderness
- Endangered Species
- Environmental
Conservation & Protection
- Essays
- Fossils
- Natural Disasters
- Natural Resources
- Plants
  - General
  - Aquatic
  - Cacti & Succulents
  - Flowers
  - Mushrooms
  - Trees
- Reference
- Regional
- rocks & Minerals
- Seashells
- Seasons
- Sky Observation
- Weather

Performing Arts
- General
- Acting & Auditioning
- Animation
- Business Aspects

- Circus
- Comedy
- Dance
  - General
  - Ballroom
  - Choreography & Dance Notation
  - Classical & Ballet
  - Folk
  - History & Criticism
  - Jazz
  - Modern
  - Popular
  - Reference
  - Tap
- Film & Video
  - General
  - Direction & Production
  - Guides & Reviews
  - History & Criticism
  - Reference
  - Screenwriting
- Individual Director
- Monologues & Scenes
- Puppets & Puppetry
- Radio
  - General
  - History & Criticism
  - Reference
- Reference
- Screenplays
- Storytelling
- Television
  - General
  - Direction & Production
  - Guides & Reviews
  - History & Criticism
  - Reference
  - Screenwriting
- Theater
  - General
  - Broadway & Musical Revue
  - Direction & Production
  - History & Criticism
  - Miming

- Playwriting
- Stagecraft

Pets
- General
- Birds
- Cats
  - General
  - Breeds
- Dogs
  - General
  - Breeds
  - Training
- Essays & Narratives
- Fish & Aquariums
- Food & Nutrition
- Horses
- Rabbits, Mice, Hamsters, Guinea Pigs, etc.
- Reference
- Reptiles, Amphibians & Terrariums

Philosophy
- General
- Aesthetics
- Buddhist
- Criticism
- Eastern
- Epistemology
- Essays
- Ethics & Moral Philosophy
- Free Will & Determinism
- Good & Evil
- Hermeneutics
- Hindu
- History & Surveys
  - General
  - Ancient & Classical
  - Medieval
  - Modern
  - Renaissance
- Language
- Logic

- Metaphysics
- Methodology
- Mind & Body
- Movements
  - General
  - Analytic
  - Critical Theory
  - Deconstruction
  - Empiricism
  - Existentialism
  - Humanism
  - Idealism
  - Phenomenology
  - Post-Structuralism
  - Pragmatism
  - Rationalism
  - Realism
  - Structuralism
  - Utilitarianism
- Political
- Reference
- Religious
- Social
- Taoist
- Zen

Photography
- General
- Annuals
- Business Aspects
- Collections, Catalogs, Exhibitions
  - General
  - Group Shows
  - Permanent Collections
- Commercial
- Criticism
- History
- Individual Photographers
  - General
  - Artists' Books
  - Essays
  - Monographs
- Photoessays & Documentaries

- Photojournalism
- Reference
- Subjects & Themes
  - General
  - Aerial
  - Architectural & Industrial
  - Celebrations & Events
  - Celebrity
    - General
    - Celebrity Photo Books
  - Children
  - Erotica
  - Fashion
  - Historical
  - Landscapes
  - Lifestyles
  - Nudes
  - Plants & Animals
  - Portraits
  - Regional
  - Sports
- Techniques
  - General
  - Cinematography & Videography
  - Color
  - Darkroom
  - Digital
  - Equipment
  - Lighting

Poetry
- General
- African
- American
  - General
  - African American
  - Asian American
  - Hispanic American
- Ancient & Classical
- Anthologies
- Asian
  - General

- Chinese
- Japanese
- Australian & Oceanian
- Canadian
- Caribbean & Latin American
- Epic
- European
  - General
  - English, Irish, Scottish, Welsh
  - French
  - German
  - Italian
  - Spanish & Portuguese
- Gay & Lesbian
- Medieval
- Middle Eastern
- Native American
- Russian & Former Soviet Union
- Subjects & Themes
  - General
  - Family
  - Inspirational & Religious
  - Love
  - Nature
  - Places
- Women Authors

Political Science
- General
- American Government
  - General
  - Executive Branch
  - Judicial Branch
  - Legislative Branch
  - Local
  - National
  - State
- Censorship
- Civics & citizenship
- Civil Rights

- Colonialism & Post-Colonialism
- Commentary & Opinion
- Comparative Politics
- Constitutions
- Essays
- Genocide & War Crimes
- Geopolitics
- Globalization
- History & Theory
- Human Rights
- Imperialism
- Intelligence & Espionage
- Intergovernmental Organizations
- International Relations
  - General
  - Arms Control
  - Diplomacy
  - Trade & Tariffs
  - Treaties
- Labor & Industrial Relations
- Law Enforcement
- NGOs
- Peace
- Political Economy
- Political Freedom
- Political Ideologies
  - General
  - Anarchism
  - Communism, Post-Communism & Socialism
  - Conservatism & Liberalism
  - Democracy
  - Fascism & Totalitarianism
  - Nationalism & Patriotism
  - Radicalism
- Political Process
  - General
  - Elections
  - Leadership
  - Political Advocacy
  - Political Parties

- ⮎ Propaganda
- ⮎ Public Affairs & Administration
- ⮎ Public Policy
    - ⮎ General
    - ⮎ City Planning & Urban Development
    - ⮎ Communication Policy
    - ⮎ Cultural Policy
    - ⮎ Economic Policy
    - ⮎ Regional Planning
    - ⮎ Science & Technology Policy
    - ⮎ Social Policy
    - ⮎ Social Security
    - ⮎ Social Services & Welfare
- ⮎ Reference
- ⮎ Security
- ⮎ Terrorism
- ⮎ Utopias
- ⮎ Women in Politics
- ⮎ World
    - ⮎ General
    - ⮎ African
    - ⮎ Asian
    - ⮎ Australian & Oceanian
    - ⮎ Canadian
    - ⮎ Caribbean & Latin American
    - ⮎ European
    - ⮎ Middle Eastern
    - ⮎ Russian & Former Soviet Union

Psychology
- ⮎ General
- ⮎ Applied Psychology
- ⮎ Assessment, Testing & Measurement
- ⮎ Clinical Psychology
- ⮎ Cognitive Neuroscience & Cognitive Neuropsychology
- ⮎ Cognitive Psychology & Cognition

- ⮎ Creative Ability
- ⮎ Developmental
    - ⮎ General
    - ⮎ adolescent
    - ⮎ Adulthood & Aging
    - ⮎ Child
    - ⮎ Lifespan Development
- ⮎ Education & Training
- ⮎ Emotions
- ⮎ Ethnopsychology
- ⮎ Experimental Psychology
- ⮎ Forensic Psychology
- ⮎ Grief & Loss
- ⮎ History
- ⮎ Human Sexuality
- ⮎ Hypnotism
- ⮎ Industrial & Organizational Psychology
- ⮎ Interpersonal Relations
- ⮎ Mental Health
- ⮎ Movements
    - ⮎ General
    - ⮎ Behaviorism
    - ⮎ Existential
    - ⮎ Gestalt
    - ⮎ Jungian
    - ⮎ Psychoanalysis
    - ⮎ Transpersonal
- ⮎ Neuropsychology
- ⮎ Personality
- ⮎ Physiological Psychology
- ⮎ Practice Management
- ⮎ Psychopathology
    - ⮎ General
    - ⮎ Addiction
    - ⮎ Anxieties & Phobias
    - ⮎ Attention-Deficit Disorder
    - ⮎ Autism Spectrum Disorders
    - ⮎ Bipolar Disorder
    - ⮎ Compulsive Behavior
    - ⮎ Depression
    - ⮎ Dissociative Identity Disorder
    - ⮎ Eating Disorders

➲ Personality Disorders
➲ Post-Traumatic Stress Disorder
➲ Schizophrenia
➲ Psychotherapy
  ➲ General
  ➲ Child & Adolescent
  ➲ Counseling
  ➲ Couples & Family
  ➲ Group
➲ Reference
➲ Research & Methodology
➲ Social Psychology
➲ Statistics
➲ Suicide

Reference
➲ General
➲ Almanacs
➲ Atlases, Gazetteers & Maps
➲ Bibliographies & Indexes
➲ Catalogs
➲ Consumer Guides
➲ Curiosities & Wonders
➲ Dictionaries
➲ Directories
➲ Encyclopedias
➲ Etiquette
➲ Genealogy & Heraldry
➲ Handbooks & Manuals
➲ Japanese Non Fiction
➲ Personal & Practical Guides
➲ Questions & Answers
➲ Quotations
➲ Research
➲ Survival & Emergency Preparedness
➲ Thesauri
➲ Trivia
➲ Weddings
➲ Word Lists
➲ Writing Skills
➲ Yearbooks & Annuals

Religion
➲ General
➲ Agnosticism
➲ Ancient
➲ Antiquities & Archaeology
➲ Atheism
➲ Baha'i
➲ Biblical Biography
  ➲ General
  ➲ New Testament
  ➲ Old Testament
➲ Biblical Commentary
  ➲ General
  ➲ New Testament
  ➲ Old Testament
➲ Biblical Criticism & Interpretation
  ➲ General
  ➲ New Testament
  ➲ Old Testament
➲ Biblical Meditations
  ➲ General
  ➲ New Testament
  ➲ Old Testament
➲ Biblical Reference
  ➲ General
  ➲ Atlases
  ➲ Concordances
  ➲ Dictionaries & Encyclopedias
  ➲ Handbooks
  ➲ Lanuage Study
  ➲ Quotations
➲ Biblical Studies
  ➲ General
  ➲ Bible Study Guides
  ➲ Exegesis & Hermeneutics
  ➲ History & Culture
  ➲ Jesus, the Gospels & Acts
  ➲ New Testament
  ➲ Old Testament
  ➲ Paul's Letters
  ➲ Prophecy
  ➲ Prophets

- ⮑ Wisdom Literature
- ⮑ Blasphemy, Heresy & Apostasy
- ⮑ Buddhism
  - ⮑ General
  - ⮑ History
  - ⮑ Rituals & Practice
  - ⮑ Sacred Writings
  - ⮑ Theravada
  - ⮑ Tibetan
  - ⮑ Zen
- ⮑ Christian Church
  - ⮑ General
  - ⮑ Administration
  - ⮑ Canon & Ecclesiastical Law
  - ⮑ Growth
  - ⮑ History
  - ⮑ Leadership
- ⮑ Christian Education
  - ⮑ General
  - ⮑ Adult
  - ⮑ Children & Youth
- ⮑ Christian Life
  - ⮑ General
  - ⮑ Death, Grief, Bereavement
  - ⮑ Devotional
  - ⮑ Family
  - ⮑ Inspirational
  - ⮑ Love & Marriage
  - ⮑ Men's Issues
  - ⮑ Personal Growth
  - ⮑ Prayer
  - ⮑ Professional Growth
  - ⮑ Relationships
  - ⮑ Social Issues
  - ⮑ Spiritual Growth
  - ⮑ Spiritual Warfare
  - ⮑ Stewardship & Giving
  - ⮑ Women's Issues
- ⮑ Christian Ministry
  - ⮑ General
  - ⮑ Adult
  - ⮑ Children
  - ⮑ Counseling & Recovery

- ⮑ Discipleship
- ⮑ Evangelism
- ⮑ Missions
- ⮑ Pastoral Resources
- ⮑ Preaching
- ⮑ Youth
- ⮑ Christian Rituals & Practice
  - ⮑ General
  - ⮑ Sacraments
  - ⮑ Worship & Liturgy
- ⮑ Christian Theology
  - ⮑ General
  - ⮑ Angelology & Demonology
  - ⮑ Anthropology
  - ⮑ Apologetics
  - ⮑ Christology
  - ⮑ Ecclesiology
  - ⮑ Eschatology
  - ⮑ Ethics
  - ⮑ History
  - ⮑ Liberation
  - ⮑ Mariology
  - ⮑ Pneumatology
  - ⮑ Process
  - ⮑ Soteriology
  - ⮑ Systematic
- ⮑ Christianity
  - ⮑ General
  - ⮑ Amish
  - ⮑ Anglican
  - ⮑ Baptist
  - ⮑ Calvinist
  - ⮑ Catechisms
  - ⮑ Catholic
  - ⮑ Christian Science
  - ⮑ Church of Jesus Christ of Latter-day Saints
  - ⮑ Denominations
  - ⮑ Episcopalian
  - ⮑ History
  - ⮑ Jehovah's Witnesses
  - ⮑ Literature & the Arts
  - ⮑ Lutheran
  - ⮑ Mennonite
  - ⮑ Methodist

- Orthodox
- Pentecostal & Charismatic
  - Presbyterian
  - Protestant
  - Quaker
  - Saints & Sainthood
  - Seventh-Day Adventist
  - Shaker
  - United Church of Christ
- Clergy
- Comparative Religion
- Confucianism
- Counseling
- Cults
- Deism
- Demonology & Satanism
- Devotional
- Eastern
- Eckankar
- Ecumenism & Interfaith
- Education
- Eschatology
- Essays
- Ethics
- Ethnic & Tribal
- Faith
- Fundamentalism
- Gnosticism
- Hinduism
  - General
  - History
  - Rituals & Practice
  - Sacred Writings
  - Theology
- History
- Holidays
  - General
  - Christian
  - Christmas & Advent
  - Easter & Lent
  - Jewish
  - Other
- Inspirational
- Institutions & Organizations
- Islam

- General
- History
- Koran & Sacred Writings
- Law
- Rituals & Practice
- Shi'a
- Sunni
- Theology
- Jainism
- Judaism
  - General
  - Conservative
  - History
  - Kabbalah & Mysticism
  - Orthodox
  - Reform
  - Rituals & Practice
  - Sacred Writings
  - Talmud
  - Theology
- Leadership
- Meditations
- Messianic Judaism
- Monasticism
- Mysticism
- Paganism & Neo-Praganism
- Philosophy
- Prayer
- Prayerbooks
  - General
  - Christian
  - Islamic
  - Jewish
- Psychology of Religion
- Reference
- Religion & Science
- Religion, Politics & State
- Religious Intolerance, Persecution & Conflict
- Scientology
- Sermons
  - General
  - Christian
  - Jewish

- Sexuality & Gender Studies
- Shintoism
- Sikhism
- Spirituality
- Taoism
- Theism
- Thoology
- Theosophy
- Unitarian Universalism
- Wicca
- Zoroastrianism

Science
- General
- Acoustics & Sound
- Applied Sciences
- Astronomy
- Biotechnology
- Chaotic Behavior in Systems
- Chemistry
  - General
  - Analytic
  - Clinical
  - Computational & Molecular Modeling
  - Environmental
  - Industrial & Technical
  - Inorganic
  - Organic
  - Physical & Theoretical
  - Toxicology
- Cognitive Science
- Cosmology
- Earth Sciences
  - General
  - Geography
  - Geology
  - Hydrology
  - Limnology
  - Meteorology & Climatology
  - Mineralogy
  - Oceanography
  - Sedimentology & Stratigraphy
  - Seismology & Volcanism
- Electron Microscopes & Microscopy
- Energy
- Environmental Science
- Essays
- Experiments & Projects
- Global Warming & Climate Change
- Gravity
- History
- Laboratory Techniques
- Life Sciences
  - General
  - Anatomy & Physiology
  - Bacteriology
  - Biochemistry
  - Biological Diversity
  - Biology
  - Biophysics
  - Botany
  - Cell Biology
  - Developmental Biology
  - Ecology
  - Evolution
  - Genetics & Genomics
  - Horticulture
  - Human Anatomy & Physiology
  - Marine Biology
  - Microbiology
  - Molecular Biology
  - Mycology
  - Neuroscience
  - Taxonomy
  - Virology
  - Zoology
    - General
    - Entomology
    - Ichthyology & Herpetology
    - Invertebrates
    - Mammals

- ⮞ Ornithology
- ⮞ Primatology
- ⮞ Mechanics
  - ⮞ General
  - ⮞ Aerodynamics
  - ⮞ Dynamics
  - ⮞ Fluids
  - ⮞ Hydrodynamics
  - ⮞ Solids
  - ⮞ Statics
  - ⮞ Thermodynamics
- ⮞ Microscopes & Microscopy
- ⮞ Nanoscience
- ⮞ Natural History
- ⮞ Paleontology
- ⮞ Philosophy & Social Aspects
- ⮞ Physics
  - ⮞ General
  - ⮞ Astrophysics
  - ⮞ Atomic & Molecular
  - ⮞ Condensed Matter
  - ⮞ Crystallography
  - ⮞ Electricity
  - ⮞ Electromagnetism
  - ⮞ Geophysics
  - ⮞ Magnetism
  - ⮞ Mathematical & Computational
  - ⮞ Nuclear
  - ⮞ Optics & Light
  - ⮞ Polymer
  - ⮞ Quantum Theory
  - ⮞ Relativity
- ⮞ Radiation
- ⮞ Radiology
- ⮞ Reference
- ⮞ Research & Methodology
- ⮞ Scientific Instruments
- ⮞ Space Science
- ⮞ Spectroscopy & Spectrum Analysis
- ⮞ Study & Teaching
- ⮞ System Theory
- ⮞ Time
- ⮞ Waves & Wave Mechanics

- ⮞ Weights & Measures

Self-Help
- ⮞ General
- ⮞ Abuse
- ⮞ Adult Children of Substance Abusers
- ⮞ Affirmations
- ⮞ Aging
- ⮞ Anger Management
- ⮞ Anxieties & Phobias
- ⮞ Codependency
- ⮞ Communication & Social Skills
- ⮞ Compulsive Behavior
  - ⮞ General
  - ⮞ Gambling
  - ⮞ Sex & Pornography Addiction
- ⮞ Creativity
- ⮞ Death, Grief, Bereavement
- ⮞ Dreams
- ⮞ Eating Disorders & Body Image
- ⮞ Emotions
- ⮞ Fashion & Style
- ⮞ Green Lifestyle
- ⮞ Handwriting Analysis
- ⮞ Meditations
- ⮞ Mood Disorders
  - ⮞ General
  - ⮞ Bipolar Disorder
  - ⮞ Depression
- ⮞ Motivational & Inspirational
- ⮞ Neuro-Linguistic Programming
- ⮞ Personal Growth
  - ⮞ General
  - ⮞ Happiness
  - ⮞ Memory Improvement
  - ⮞ Self-Esteem
  - ⮞ Success
- ⮞ Port-Traumatic Stress Disorder (PTSD)
- ⮞ Self Hypnosis

- Self Management
  - General
  - Stress Management
  - Time Management
- Sexual Instruction
- Spiritual
- Substance Abuse & Addictions
  - General
  - Tobacco
- Twelve-Step Programs

Social Science
- General
- Abortion & Birth Control
- Agriculture & Food
- Anthropology
  - General
  - Cultural
  - Physical
- Archaeology
- Black Studies
- Body Language & Nonverbal Communication
- Children's Studies
- Conspiracy Theories
- Criminology
- Customs & Traditions
- Death & Dying
- Demography
- Developing & Emerging Countries
- Disasters & Disaster Relief
- Discrimination & Race Relations
- Disease & Health Issues
- Emigration & Immigration
- Essays
- Ethnic Studies
  - General
  - African American Studies
  - Asian American Studies

- Hispanic American Studies
- Native American Studies
- Feminism & Feminist Theory
- Folklore & Mythology
- Freemasonry & Secret Societies
- Future Studies
- Gay Studies
- Gender Studies
- Gerontology
- Holidays
- Human Geography
- Human Services
- Indigenous Studies
- Islamic Studies
- Jewish Studies
- Lesbian Studies
- Media Studies
- Men's Studies
- Methodology
- Minority Studies
- Penology
- People with Disabilities
- Philanthropy & Charity
- Popular Culture
- Pornography
- Poverty & Homelessness
- Prostitution & Sex Trade
- Reference
- Regional Studies
- Research
- Sexual Abuse & Harassment
- Slavery
- Social Classes
- Social Work
- Sociology
  - General
  - Marriage & Family
  - Rural
  - Urban
- Sociology of Religion
- Statistics

- Violence in Society
- Volunteer Work
- Women's Studies

Sports & Recreation
- General
- Air Sports
- Archery
- Baseball
- Basketball
  - General
  - Essays & Writing
  - History
  - Statistics
- Boating
- Bodybuilding & Weight Training
- Bowling
- Boxing
- Business Aspects
- Camping
- Canoeing
- Caving
- Cheerleading
- Coaching
  - General
  - Baseball
  - Basketball
  - Football
  - Soccer
- Cricket
- Cycling
- Dog Racing
- Equestrian
- Equipment & Supplies
- Essays
- Extreme Sports
- Fencing
- Field Hockey
- Fishing
- Football
- Golf
- Gymnastics
- Health & Safety
- Hiking

- History
- Hockey
- Horse Racing
- Hunting
- Ice & Figure Skating
- Juggling
- Kayaking
- Lacrosse
- Martial Arts & Self-Defense
- Motor Sports
- Mountaineering
- Olympics
- Outdoor Skills
- Polo
- Pool, Billiards, Snooker
- Racket Sports
- Racquetball
- Reference
- Rodeos
- Roller & In-Line Skating
- Rugby
- Running & Jogging
- Sailing
- Scuba & Snorkeling
- Shooting
- Skateboarding
- Skiing
- Snowboarding
- Soccer
- Sociology of Sports
- Softball
- Sports Psychology
- Squash
- Surfing
- Swimming & Diving
- Table Tennis
- Tennis
- Track & Field
- Training
- Triathlon
- Volleyball
- Walking
- Water Sports
- Winter Sports
- Wrestling

Study Aids
- ⊃ General
- ⊃ ACT
- ⊃ Advanced Placement
- ⊃ Armed Forces
- ⊃ Bar Exam
- ⊃ Book Notes
- ⊃ Citizenship
- ⊃ Civil Service
- ⊃ CLEP
- ⊃ College Entrance
- ⊃ College Guides
- ⊃ CPA
- ⊃ Financial Aid
- ⊃ GED
- ⊃ GMAT
- ⊃ Graduate School Guides
- ⊃ GRE
- ⊃ High School Entrance
- ⊃ LSAT
- ⊃ MAT
- ⊃ MCAT
- ⊃ NTE
- ⊃ Professional
- ⊃ PSAT & NMSQT
- ⊃ Regents
- ⊃ SAT
- ⊃ Study Guides
- ⊃ Tests
- ⊃ TOEFL
- ⊃ Vocational

Technology & Engineering
- ⊃ General
- ⊃ Acoustics & Sound
- ⊃ Aeronautics & Astronautics
- ⊃ Agriculture
    - ⊃ General
    - ⊃ Agronomy
        - ⊃ General
        - ⊃ Crop Science
        - ⊃ Soil Science
    - ⊃ Animal Husbandry
    - ⊃ Beekeeping

- ⊃ Enology & Viticulture
- ⊃ Forestry
- ⊃ Irrigation
- ⊃ Organic
- ⊃ Sustainable Agriculture
- ⊃ Tropical Agriculture
- ⊃ Automation
- ⊃ Automotive
- ⊃ Biomedical
- ⊃ Cartography
- ⊃ Chemical & Biochemical
- ⊃ Civil
    - ⊃ General
    - ⊃ Bridges
    - ⊃ Dams & Reservoirs
    - ⊃ Earthquake
    - ⊃ Flood Control
    - ⊃ Highway & Traffic
    - ⊃ Soil & Rock
    - ⊃ Transport
- ⊃ Construction
    - ⊃ General
    - ⊃ Carpentry
    - ⊃ Contracting
    - ⊃ Electrical
    - ⊃ Estimating
    - ⊃ Heating, Ventilation & Air Conditioning
    - ⊃ Masonry
    - ⊃ Plumbing
    - ⊃ Roofing
- ⊃ Drafting & Mechanical Drawing
- ⊃ Electrical
- ⊃ Electronics
    - ⊃ General
    - ⊃ Circuits
        - ⊃ General
        - ⊃ Integrated
        - ⊃ Logic
        - ⊃ VLSE & ULSI
    - ⊃ Digital
    - ⊃ Microelectronics
    - ⊃ Optoelectronics
    - ⊃ Semiconductors
    - ⊃ Solid State

- ➲ Transistors
- ➲ Emergency Management
- ➲ Engineering
- ➲ Environmental
  - ➲ General
  - ➲ Pollution Control
  - ➲ Waste Management
  - ➲ Water Supply
- ➲ Fiber Optics
- ➲ Fire Science
- ➲ Fisheries & Aquaculture
- ➲ Food Science
- ➲ Fracture Mechanics
- ➲ History
- ➲ Holography
- ➲ Hydraulics
- ➲ Imaging Systems
- ➲ Industrial Design
  - ➲ General
  - ➲ Packaging
  - ➲ Product
- ➲ Industrial Engineering
- ➲ Industrial Health & Safety
- ➲ Industrial Technology
- ➲ Inventions
- ➲ Lasers & Photonics
- ➲ Machinery
- ➲ Manufacturing
- ➲ Marine & Naval
- ➲ Materials Science
- ➲ Measurement
- ➲ Mechanical
- ➲ Metallurgy
- ➲ Microwaves
- ➲ Military Science
- ➲ Mining
- ➲ Mobile & Wireless Communications
- ➲ Nanotechnology & MEMS
- ➲ Operations Research
- ➲ Optics
- ➲ Pest Control
- ➲ Petroleum
- ➲ Power Resources
  - ➲ General

- ➲ Alternative & Renewable
  - ➲ Electrical
  - ➲ Fossil Fuels
  - ➲ Nuclear
- ➲ Project Management
- ➲ Quality Control
- ➲ Radar
- ➲ Radio
- ➲ Reference
- ➲ Remote Sensing & Geographic Information Systems
- ➲ Research
- ➲ Robotics
- ➲ Sensors
- ➲ Signals & Signal Processing
- ➲ Social Aspects
- ➲ Structural
- ➲ Superconductors & Superconductivity
- ➲ Surveying
- ➲ Technical & Manufacturing Industries & Trades
- ➲ Technical Writing
- ➲ Telecommunications
- ➲ Television & Video
- ➲ Textiles & Polymers
- ➲ Tribology

Transportation
- ➲ General
- ➲ Automotive
  - ➲ General
  - ➲ Antique & Classic
  - ➲ Buyer's Guides
  - ➲ Customizing
  - ➲ History
  - ➲ Pictorial
  - ➲ Repair & Maintenance
  - ➲ Trucks
- ➲ Aviation
  - ➲ General
  - ➲ Commercial

- ⊃ History
- ⊃ Piloting & Flight Instruction
- ⊃ Repair & Maintenance
- ⊃ Bicycles
- ⊃ Motorcycles
  - ⊃ General
  - ⊃ History
  - ⊃ Pictorial
  - ⊃ Repair & Maintenance
- ⊃ Navigation
- ⊃ Public Transportation
- ⊃ Railroads
  - ⊃ General
  - ⊃ History
  - ⊃ Pictorial
- ⊃ Ships & Shipbuilding
  - ⊃ General
  - ⊃ History
  - ⊃ Pictorial
  - ⊃ Repair & Maintenance

Travel
- ⊃ General
- ⊃ Africa
  - ⊃ General
  - ⊃ Central
  - ⊃ East
  - ⊃ Kenya
  - ⊃ Morocco
  - ⊃ North
  - ⊃ Republic of South Africa
  - ⊃ South
  - ⊃ West
- ⊃ Amusement & Theme Parks
- ⊃ Asia
  - ⊃ General
  - ⊃ Central
  - ⊃ China
  - ⊃ Far East
  - ⊃ India & South Asia
  - ⊃ Japan
  - ⊃ Southeast

- ⊃ Southwest
- ⊃ Australian & Oceania
- ⊃ Bed & Breakfast
- ⊃ Budget
- ⊃ Canada
  - ⊃ General
  - ⊃ Atlantic Provinces
  - ⊃ Ontario
  - ⊃ Prairie Provinces
  - ⊃ Quebec
  - ⊃ Territories & Nunavut
  - ⊃ Western Provinces
- ⊃ Caribbean & West Indies
- ⊃ Central America
- ⊃ Cruises
- ⊃ Essays & Travelogues
- ⊃ Europe
  - ⊃ General
  - ⊃ Austria
  - ⊃ Benelux Countries
  - ⊃ Cyprus
  - ⊃ Denmark
  - ⊃ Eastern
  - ⊃ France
  - ⊃ Germany
  - ⊃ Great Britain
  - ⊃ Greece
  - ⊃ Iceland & Greenland
  - ⊃ Ireland
  - ⊃ Italy
  - ⊃ Scandinavia
  - ⊃ Spain & Portugal
  - ⊃ Switzerland
  - ⊃ Western
- ⊃ Former Soviet Republics
- ⊃ Hikes & Walks
- ⊃ Hotels, Inns & Hostels
- ⊃ Maps & Road Atlases
- ⊃ Mexico
- ⊃ Middle East
  - ⊃ General
  - ⊃ Egypt
  - ⊃ Israel
  - ⊃ Turkey
- ⊃ Museums, Tours, Points of Interest

- Parks & Campgrounds
- Pictorials
- Polar Regions
- Rail Travel
- Reference
- Resorts & Spas
- Restaurants
- Road Travel
- Russia
- Shopping
- South America
  - General
  - Argentina
  - Brazil
  - Chile & Easter Island
  - Ecuador & Galapagos Islands
  - Peru
- Special Interest
  - General
  - Adventure
  - Business
  - Ecotourism
  - Family
  - LGBT
  - Literary
  - Pets
  - Religious
  - Senior
  - Sports
- United States
  - General
  - Midwest
    - General

- East North Central
- West North Central
- Northeast
  - General
  - Middle Atlantic
  - New England
- South
  - General
  - East South Central
  - South Atlantic
  - West South Central
- West
  - General
  - Mountain
  - Pacific

True Crime
- General
- Espionage
- Hoaxes & Deceptions
- Murder
  - General
  - Serial Killers
- Organized Crime
- White Collar Crime

Non Classifiable

Appendix D
Sub Categories - Fiction

Children's sub category keywords

Sub Category	Keywords
Children's Age Range/ Baby-2	baby
Children's Age Range/ Ages 3-5	preschool
Children's Age Range/ Ages 6-8	ages 6-8
Children's Age Range/ 9-12	preteen
Children's Fantasy & Magic/Coming of Age	coming of age
Children's Fantasy & Magic/Sword & Sorcery	sword, sorcery, magic, dragon, quest
Children's Mystery & Thrillers/Detectives	detective, sleuth
Children's Mystery & Thrillers/Fantasy & Supernatural	fantasy, paranormal, magic
Children's Mystery & Thrillers/Spies	spy, terrorist, secret agent
Children's Science Fiction/Action & Adventure	action, adventure
Children's Science Fiction/Action & Adventure/Superheroes	superhero
Children's Science Fiction/Aliens	alien, extraterrestrial
Children's Science Fiction/Time Travel	time travel

Romance sub category keywords

Sub Category	Keywords
Romance/Holidays*	christmas, thanksgiving, valentine, halloween, new year

Romance/Inspirational/Amish*	amish
Romance/Inspirational/General*	inspirational
Romance/Military	military, navy, army, soldier
Romance/Multicultural & Interracial	interracial
Romance/New Adult & College	new adult
Romance/Paranormal/Angels	angel
Romance/Paranormal/Demons & Devils	devil, demon
Romance/Paranormal/Ghosts	ghost, spirit
Romance/Paranormal/Psychics	psychic, telepathy
Romance/Paranormal/Vampires	vampire
Romance/Paranormal/Werewolves & Shifters	werewolf, shapeshifter
Romance/Paranormal/Witches & Wizards	witch, wizard, warlock, druid, shaman
Romance/Romantic Comedy	comedy, humor
Romance/Sports*	sport, hockey, soccer, baseball, basketball, football, olympics, climbing, lacrosse, nascar, surfing, boxing, martial arts, golf
Romantic Heroes/Cowboys	cowboy
Romantic Heroes/Doctors	doctor, physician, surgeon
Romantic Heroes/Firefighters	firefighter
Romantic Heroes/Highlanders	highlander
Romantic Heroes/Pirates	pirate
Romantic Heroes/Politicians	politician
Romantic Heroes/Rich & Wealthy	billionaire, rich, millionaire, wealthy
Romantic Heroes/Royalty & Aristocrats	nobility, royalty, aristocrat, prince
Romantic Heroes/Spies	spies, espionage
Romantic Heroes/Vikings	viking
Romantic Themes/Amnesia	amnesia
Romantic Themes/Beaches	beach
Romantic Themes/Gambling &	gambling, poker, casino

Poker	
Romantic Themes/International	international
Romantic Themes/Love Triangle	love triangle, menage
Romantic Themes/Medical	medical, doctor, nurse, hospital
Romantic Themes/Second Chances	second chance
Romantic Themes/Secret Baby	baby, pregnancy
Romantic Themes/Vacation	vacation
Romantic Themes/Wedding	wedding
Romantic Themes/Workplace	office, workplace

*Subcategory is specific to the U.S. marketplace or Amazon.com

Teen & Young Adult sub category keywords

Sub Category	Keywords
Children's & Teen's Horror Characters/Angels & Demons	angels
Children's & Teen's Horror Characters/Ghosts	ghosts
Children's & Teen's Horror Characters/Vampires	vampires
Children's & Teen's Horror Characters/Werewolves & Shifters	werewolf, shapeshifters
Children's & Teen's Horror Characters/Witches & Wizards	witch, wizard, warlock, druid, shaman
Children's & Teen's Horror Characters/Zombies	zombies
Teen & Young Adult Fantasy/Coming of Age	coming of age
Teen & Young Adult Fantasy/Sword & Sorcery	sword, sorcery, magic, dragon, quest
Teen & Young Adult Mystery/Detectives	detective, sleuth
Teen & Young Adult Mystery/Fantasy & Supernatural	fantasy, paranormal, magic
Teen & Young Adult Mystery/Romantic	love, romantic

Teen & Young Adult Mystery/Science Fiction	science fiction, dystopian
Teen & Young Adult Mystery/Spies	spy, terrorist, secret agent
Teen & Young Adult Romance/Historical	historical
Teen & Young Adult Romance/Fantasy & Paranormal	fantasy, paranormal, magic
Teen & Young Adult Romance/Science Fiction & Dystopian	science fiction, dystopian
Teen & Young Adult Science Fiction/Action & Adventure	action, adventure
Teen & Young Adult Science Fiction/Aliens	alien, extraterrestrial
Teen & Young Adult Science Fiction/Time Travel	time travel

Comics & Graphic Novels sub category keywords

Sub Category	Keywords
Comics & Graphic Novels/General/Action	action, adventure
Comics & Graphic Novels/General/Art	art
Comics & Graphic Novels/General/Comedy	comedy, humor
Comics & Graphic Novels/General/Holiday	holiday, christmas, thanksgiving, valentine, halloween, new year
Comics & Graphic Novels/General/Military	military
Comics & Graphic Novels/General/Mystery, Thriller, Suspense	mystery, thriller, suspense
Comics & Graphic Novels/General/Pulp	pulp
Comics & Graphic Novels/General/Sampler	sampler

Comics & Graphic Novels/General/Single Issue	single issue
Comics & Graphic Novels/General/Sports	sport, hockey, soccer, baseball, basketball, football, olympics, climbing, lacrosse, nascar, surfing, boxing, martial arts, golf
Comics & Graphic Novels/General/Western	westerns
Comics & Graphic Novels/General/Zombies	zombies
Comics & Graphic Novels/Manga/General/Action	action, adventure
Comics & Graphic Novels/Manga/General/Comedy	comedy, humor
Comics & Graphic Novels/Manga/General/Military	military
Comics & Graphic Novels/Manga/General/Harem	harem
Comics & Graphic Novels/Manga/General/Shojo	shojo
Comics & Graphic Novels/Manga/General/Shounen	shounen
Comics Publication Era/Platinum Age (1897-1937)	platinum age
Comics Publication Era/Golden Age (1938-55)	golden age
Comics Publication Era/Silver Age (1956-69)	silver age
Comics Publication Era/Bronze Age (1970-83)	bronze age
Comics Publication Era/Copper Age (1984-1991)	copper age
Comics Publication Era/Modern Age (1992-Now)	modern age

Science Fiction & Fantasy sub category keywords

Sub Category	Keywords

Fantasy Characters/Angels	angels
Fantasy Characters/Devils & Demons	demons
Fantasy Characters/Dragons	dragons
Fantasy Characters/Elves & Fae	elf, fae, fairies
Fantasy Characters/Ghosts	ghost, spirit
Fantasy Characters/Gods & Goddesses	deities, god, pantheon
Fantasy Characters/Psychics	psychic, telepathic
Fantasy Characters/Vampires	vampire
Fantasy Characters/Werewolves & Shifters	shapeshifter
Fantasy Characters/Witches & Wizards	witch, wizard, warlock, druid, shaman
Science Fiction Characters/AIs	artificial intelligence
Science Fiction Characters/Aliens	aliens
Science Fiction Characters/Clones	clones
Science Fiction Characters/Corporations	corporations
Science Fiction Characters/Mutants	mutants
Science Fiction Characters/Pirates	pirates, privateer, corsair
Science Fiction Characters/Psychics	psychics
Science Fiction Characters/Robots & Androids	robots, androids
Science Fiction & Fantasy/Horror	horror
Science Fiction & Fantasy/Humor	humor
Science Fiction & Fantasy/Mystery	mystery
Science Fiction & Fantasy/Non-Romantic	Do NOT include "romance" or "love"
Science Fiction & Fantasy/Romantic	romance, love
Science Fiction & Fantasy/Thriller	thriller
Science Fiction & Fantasy/Fantasy/Arthurian	arthurian

Science Fiction & Fantasy/Fantasy/Coming of Age	coming of age
Science Fiction & Fantasy/Fantasy/Metaphysical & Visionary	metaphysical, visionary, theology, sprititual
Science Fiction & Fantasy/Fantasy/Myths & Legends/Arthurian	arthurian, camelot, merlin, excalibur, lancelot
Science Fiction & Fantasy/Fantasy/Myths & Legends/Greek & Roman	greek, roman, zeus, apollo, athena, olympus
Science Fiction & Fantasy/Fantasy/Myths & Legends/Norse & Viking	viking, norse, nordic, finland, swedish, thor, odin
Science Fiction & Fantasy/Fantasy/Superhero	superhero
Science Fiction & Fantasy/Fantasy/Sword & Sorcery	sword, sorcery, magic, dragon, quest
Science Fiction & Fantasy/Science Fiction/Alien Invasion	invasion
Science Fiction & Fantasy/Science Fiction/Colonization	colonization
Science Fiction & Fantasy/Science Fiction/Cyberpunk	cyberpunk
Science Fiction & Fantasy/Science Fiction/First Contact	contact
Science Fiction & Fantasy/Science Fiction/Galactic Empire	empire, republic
Science Fiction & Fantasy/Science Fiction/Genetic Engineering	genes
Science Fiction & Fantasy/Science Fiction/Metaphysical & Visionary	metaphysical, visionary, theology, spiritual
Science Fiction &	fleet, starship

Fantasy/Science Fiction/Military/Space Fleet	
Science Fiction & Fantasy/Science Fiction/Military/Space Marine	troop, armor, marine, soldier
Science Fiction & Fantasy/Science Fiction/Space Exploration	exploration

Mystery, Thriller, & Suspense sub category keywords

For authors in the UK: This category is known as "Crime, Mystery, & Thriller," and includes keywords that apply only on Amazon.co.uk. They're noted at the bottom of the chart.

Sub Category	Keywords
Mystery, Thriller & Suspense Characters/Amateur Sleuth	amateur
Mystery, Thriller & Suspense Characters/British Detectives	british detective
Mystery, Thriller & Suspense Characters/FBI Agents	fbi
Mystery, Thriller & Suspense Characters/Female Protagonists	female protagonist
Mystery, Thriller & Suspense Characters/Police Officers	police
Mystery, Thriller & Suspense Characters/Private Investigators	private investigator
Mystery, Thriller & Suspense/Crime Fiction/Heist	heist, robbery, thief, theft
Mystery, Thriller & Suspense/Crime Fiction/Murder	murder
Mystery, Thriller & Suspense/Crime Fiction/Noir	noir
Mystery, Thriller & Suspense/Crime Fiction/Organized Crime	mob, mafia, organized crime, yakuza
Mystery, Thriller & Suspense/Crime Fiction/Serial Killers	serial killer

Mystery, Thriller & Suspense/Crime Fiction/Vigilante Justice	vigilante justice
Mystery, Thriller & Suspense Moods/Dark	dark
Mystery, Thriller & Suspense Moods/Disturbing	disturbing
Mystery, Thriller & Suspense Moods/Fun	fun
Mystery, Thriller & Suspense Moods/Humorous	comedy
Mystery, Thriller & Suspense Moods/Racy	racy
Mystery, Thriller & Suspense Moods/Scary	scary
Mystery, Thriller & Suspense Moods/Vengeful	vengeful
Mystery, Thriller & Suspense/Mystery/Cozy/Animals	cat, dog, horse, animal, pets
Mystery, Thriller & Suspense/Mystery/Cozy/Crafts & Hobbies	craft, hobby, knitting, quilting
Mystery, Thriller & Suspense/Mystery/Cozy/Culinary	food, cook, bake
Mystery, Thriller & Suspense Settings/Beaches	beach
Mystery, Thriller & Suspense Settings/Islands	island
Mystery, Thriller & Suspense Settings/Mountains	mountain
Mystery, Thriller & Suspense Settings/Outer Space	space
Mystery, Thriller & Suspense Settings/Small Towns	small town
Mystery, Thriller & Suspense Settings/Suburban	suburban
Mystery, Thriller & Suspense Settings/Urban	urban

Mystery, Thriller & Suspense/Suspense/Paranormal/General	paranormal
Mystery, Thriller & Suspense/Suspense/Paranormal/Psychics	psychic, telepathy
Mystery, Thriller & Suspense/Suspense/Paranormal/Vampires	vampire
Mystery, Thriller & Suspense/Suspense/Paranormal/Werewolves & Shifters	werewolf, shapeshifter
Mystery, Thriller & Suspense/Thrillers/Assassinations	assassin, hitman
Mystery, Thriller & Suspense/Thrillers/Conspiracies	conspiracy
Mystery, Thriller & Suspense/Thrillers/Financial	financial
Mystery, Thriller & Suspense/Thrillers/Pulp	pulp
Mystery, Thriller & Suspense/Thrillers/Terrorism	terrorism
UK-specific keywords:	
Crime, Thriller & Mystery / Crime Fiction / British & Irish / English	london, england, english
Crime, Thriller & Mystery / Crime Fiction / British & Irish / Irish	ireland, dublin, ira, irish
Crime, Thriller & Mystery / Crime Fiction / British & Irish / Northern Irish	northern ireland, northern irish, belfast
Crime, Thriller & Mystery / Crime Fiction / British & Irish / Scottish	scotland, scottish, edinburgh, glasgow
Crime, Thriller & Mystery / Crime Fiction / British & Irish / Welsh	wales, welsh, cardiff
Crime, Thriller & Mystery / Crime Fiction / Scandinavian	scandinavian, scandinavia, sweden, swedish, stockholm, norway, norwegian, oslo, denmark, danish, stockholm, nordic

Literature & Fiction sub category keywords

Sub Category	Keywords
Historical Fiction Time Periods/Ancient	ancient
Historical Fiction Time Periods/Medieval	medieval
Historical Fiction Time Periods/Renaissance	renaissance
Historical Fiction Time Periods/16th Century	16th century
Historical Fiction Time Periods/17th Century	17th century
Historical Fiction Time Periods/18th Century	18th century
Historical Fiction Time Periods/19th Century	19th century
Historical Fiction Time Periods/20th Century	20th century
Historical Fiction Time Periods/21st Century	21st century
Literary Fiction Themes/Aging	aging, aged
Literary Fiction Themes/Childhood	childhood, youth
Literary Fiction Themes/Coming of Age	coming of age
Literary Fiction Themes/Death & Grief	death, loss, grief
Literary Fiction Themes/Depression & Mental Illness	depression, mental illness
Literary Fiction Themes/Alcohol & Drug Abuse	alcohol abuse, drug abuse
Literary Fiction Themes/Family Life	family life
Literary Fiction Themes/Friendship	friendship
Literary Fiction Themes/Immigration	immigration, immigrant

Literary Fiction Themes/Love Stories	love
Literary Fiction Themes/Marriage	marriage
Literary Fiction Themes/Politics	politics, politician
Literary Fiction Themes/Religion	religion, religious, spiritual
Literary Fiction Themes/Travel	travel, voyage
Literary Fiction Themes/Military & War	military, war
Literary Fiction Themes/School & College	military & war
Women's Fiction Themes/Career & Workplace	career, workplace, working, office
Women's Fiction Themes/Divorce	divorce
Women's Fiction Themes/Marriage	marriage
Women's Fiction Themes/Family Life	family life
Women's Fiction Themes/Friendship	friendship
Women's Fiction Themes/Parenthood & Children	parenting, parent and children
Women's Fiction Themes/Dating & Relationships	dating, relationships
Women's Fiction Themes/Singlehood	singlehood, single women
Women's Fiction Themes/Sisterhood	sister
Women's Fiction Themes/Weddings	wedding

Erotica sub category keywords

Sub Category	Keywords
Erotica/Action & Adventure	action, adventure, pulp
Erotica/Adult Fairy Tales	fairy tales
Erotica/BDSM	bdsm, bondage, sadism, masochism, submission

Erotica/Historical	historical
Erotica/Horror	horror
Erotica/Humorous	humor, humour, comedy
Erotica/Interracial	interracial
Erotica/LGBT/Bisexual	bisexual
Erotica/LGBT/Gay	gay
Erotica/LGBT/Lesbian	lesbian
Erotica/LGBT/Transgender	transgender
Erotica/Mystery	mystery
Erotica/Paranormal	paranormal
Erotica/Poetry	poetry, poem
Erotica/Romantic Erotica	romance
Erotica/Science Fiction	science fiction
Erotica/Suspense	suspense
Erotica/Thrillers	thriller
Erotica/Urban	urban
Erotica/Victorian	victorian
Erotica/Westerns	western
Erotica: Erotica Characters/Alpha Males	alpha male
Erotica: Erotica Characters/Angels	angel
Erotica: Erotica Characters/BBW	bbw, rubenesque
Erotica: Erotica Characters/Bikers	motorcycle, biker
Erotica: Erotica Characters/Billionaires	billionaire
Erotica: Erotica Characters/Cowboys	cowboy
Erotica: Erotica Characters/Devils & Demons	devil, demon
Erotica: Erotica Characters/Ghosts	ghost, spirit
Erotica: Erotica Characters/People in Uniform	uniform, police, military, nurse, maid, combat, doctor
Erotica: Erotica Characters/Rockstars	rock

Erotica: Erotica Characters/Shapeshifters	shifter
Erotica: Erotica Characters/Vampires	vampire
Erotica: Erotica Characters/Werewolves	werewolf
Erotica/Action & Adventure	action, adventure, pulp
Erotica/Adult Fairy Tales	fairy tales

Appendix E
Sub Categories - Non Fiction

Religion & Spirituality sub category keywords

Sub Category	Keywords
Religion & Spirituality/Christian Books & Bibles/Bibles/More Translations/Evangelical	evangelical
Religion & Spirituality/Christian Books & Bibles/Bibles/More Translations/Life Application	life application
Religion & Spirituality/Christian Books & Bibles/Bibles/More Translations/Spanish Language	spanish
Religion & Spirituality/Christian Books & Bibles//Catholicism/Inspirational	inspire, inspires, inspiration, inspirational
Religion & Spirituality/Christian Books & Bibles/Catholicism/Popes & the Vatican	papal, papacy, pope, popes, vatican
Religion & Spirituality/Christian Books & Bibles/Catholicism/Roman Catholicism	roman catholic, roman catholics, roman catholicism
Religion & Spirituality/Christian Books & Bibles/Catholicism/Self-Help	self-help, self help
Religion & Spirituality/Christian Books & Bibles/Christian Fiction/Poetry	christian poetry
Religion & Spirituality/Christian Books & Bibles/Christian Living/Counseling	christian, christianity
Religion & Spirituality/Christian Books & Bibles/Christian Living/Music/Hymns	christian, christians, christianity

Religion & Spirituality/Christian Books & Bibles/Christian Living/Self-Help	self-help, self help
Religion & Spirituality/Christian Books & Bibles/History/Historical Jesus	historical jesus
Religion & Spirituality/Christian Books & Bibles/Protestantism/Inspirational	inspire, inspires, inspiration, inspirational
Religion & Spirituality/Christian Books & Bibles/Protestantism/Self-Help	self-help, self help
Religion & Spirituality/Christian Books & Bibles/Theology/Catholic	catholic, catholics, catholicism
Religion & Spirituality/Christian Books & Bibles/Theology/Creationism	creationism
Religion & Spirituality/Christian Books & Bibles/Theology/Prophecy	prophecy
Religion & Spirituality/Christian Books & Bibles/Worship & Devotion/Book of Common Prayer	book of common prayer
Religion & Spirituality/Christian Books & Bibles/Worship & Devotion/Meditations	meditation, meditations, meditating
Religion & Spirituality/Earth-Based Religions/Druidism	druid, druids, druidism
Religion & Spirituality/Hinduism/Bhagavad Gita	bhagavad gita
Religion & Spirituality/Hinduism/Sanskrit	sanskrit
Religion & Spirituality/Hinduism/Upanishads	upanishads
Religion & Spirituality/Islam/Muhammad	muhammad, muhammed, mohammed
Religion & Spirituality/Islam/Women in Islam	woman, women

Religion & Spirituality/Earth-Based Religions/Druidism	druid, druids, druidism
Religion & Spirituality/Judaism/Hasidism	hasidic, hasidism
Religion & Spirituality/Judaism/Sacred Writings/Hebrew Bible (Old Testament)/Hebrew	hebrew
Religion & Spirituality/New Age/Chakras	chakra, chakras
Religion & Spirituality/New Age/Self-Help	new age
Religion & Spirituality/New Age/Urantia	urantia
Religion & Spirituality/Occult/Alchemy	alchemy, alchemic, alchemical, alchemist, alchemists
Religion & Spirituality/Occult/Ghosts & Haunted Houses/Ghosts	ghost, ghosts
Religion & Spirituality/Occult/Ghosts & Haunted Houses/Haunted Houses	haunted house, haunted houses
Religion & Spirituality/Occult/Metaphysical Phenomena	metaphysical, metaphysics
Religion & Spirituality/Other Eastern Religions & Sacred Texts/Book of the Dead (Tibetan)	book of the dead, tibetan book of the dead
Religion & Spirituality/Other Eastern Religions & Sacred Texts/Gurus	guru, gurus
Religion & Spirituality/Other Eastern Religions & Sacred Texts/Tao Te Ching	tao te ching
Religion & Spirituality/Spirituality/Gifts	spiritual gift, spiritual gifts
Religion & Spirituality/Spirituality/Inspirational/Conduct of Life	conduct of life

Religion & Spirituality/Spirituality/Inspirational/Death & Grief	death, dying, grief, bereavement
Religion & Spirituality/Spirituality/Inspirational/Family	family
Religion & Spirituality/Spirituality/Inspirational/Health	health, healthy, sickness, sick, illness
Religion & Spirituality/Spirituality/Inspirational/Men's Inspirational	man, men
Religion & Spirituality/Spirituality/Inspirational/Miracles	miracle, miracles
Religion & Spirituality/Spirituality/Inspirational/Personal Testimonies	personal testimony, personal testimonies
Religion & Spirituality/Spirituality/Inspirational/Relationships	relationship, relationships, dating
Religion & Spirituality/Spirituality/Inspirational/Women's Inspirational	woman, women
Religion & Spirituality/Spirituality/Personal Growth/Astrology	astrology, astrological, horoscope, horoscopes
Religion & Spirituality/Spirituality/Personal Growth/Family	interview, interviews, interviewing
Religion & Spirituality/Spirituality/Personal Growth/Men's Personal Growth	family
Religion & Spirituality/Spirituality/Personal Growth/Motivational	man, men
Religion & Spirituality/Spirituality/Personal Growth/Mysticism	motivation, motivational
Religion &	mystic, mystics, mysticism

Spirituality/Spirituality/Personal Growth/Personal Success	
Religion & Spirituality/Spirituality/Personal Growth/Philosophy	philosophy, philosophical
Religion & Spirituality/Spirituality/Personal Growth/Self-Help	self-help, self help
Religion & Spirituality/Spirituality/Personal Growth/Spiritual Healing	healing
Religion & Spirituality/Spirituality/Personal Growth/Transformational	transformation, transformations, transformational
Religion & Spirituality/Spirituality/Personal Growth/Women's Personal Growth	woman, women
Religion & Spirituality/Spirituality/Women	woman, women

Business & Money sub category keywords

Sub Category	Keywords
Business & Money/Entrepreneurship & Small Business/Startups	startup, startups
Business & Money/Technology/Big Data	big data
Business & Money/Technology/Innovation	innovation, innovations, innovating, innovator, innovators, innovate
Business & Money/Management & Leadership/Teams	team, teams
Business & Money/Economics/Unemployment	unemployment, unemployed
Business & Money/Education & Reference/MBA	MBA
Business & Money/Investing/Investing Basics	investing basics, basics

Business & Money/Job Hunting & Careers/Interviewing	interview, interviews, interviewing
Business & Money/Industries/E-commerce/Online Banking	online banking, banking online
Business & Money/Industries/Insurance/Business	business
Business & Money/Biographies & Primers/Inspiration	inspiration, inspirational
Business & Money/Business Life/Fashion & Image	fashion, image
Business & Money/Business Life/Health & Stress	health, stress
Business & Money/Personal Finance/Financial Planning	financial planning
Business & Money/Entrepreneurship & Small Business/Legal Guides	legal guides

Biographies & Memoirs Category Keywords

For authors in the UK: This category is known as "Biography & True Accounts," and includes keywords that apply only on Amazon.co.uk. They're noted at the bottom of the chart.

Sub Category	Keywords
Biographies & Memoirs/Arts & Literature/Entertainers/Actors & Actresses	actor, actors, actress, actresses
Biographies & Memoirs/Arts & Literature/Entertainers/Comedians	comedy, comedian, comedians
Biographies & Memoirs/Arts & Literature/Composers & Musicians/Punk Rock	punk rock, punk rocker
Biographies & Memoirs/Arts & Literature/Composers & Musicians/Rap & Hip-Hop	rap, rapper, hip-hop, hip hop
Biographies & Memoirs/Arts & Literature/Movie Directors	film director, cinema director, movie director, motion picture director
Biographies & Memoirs/Historical/Africa	africa, african

Biographies & Memoirs/Historical/Asia	asia, asian
Biographies & Memoirs/Historical/Canada	canada, canadian
Biographies & Memoirs/Historical/Europe/France	france, french
Biographies & Memoirs/Historical/Europe/General	europe, european
Biographies & Memoirs/Historical/Europe/Germany	germany, german
Biographies & Memoirs/Historical/Europe/Greece	greece, greek
Biographies & Memoirs/Historical/Europe/Ireland	ireland, irish, celtic
Biographies & Memoirs/Historical/Europe/Italy & Rome	italy, italian, rome, roman
Biographies & Memoirs/Historical/Europe/Russia	russia, russian
Biographies & Memoirs/Historical/Europe/Spain & Portugal	spain, spanish, portugal, portuguese
Biographies & Memoirs/Historical/Latin America	latin america, latin american, mexico, mexican, south america, south american
Biographies & Memoirs/Historical/Middle East	middle east, middle eastern, egypt, egyptian, iran, iranian, iraq, iraqi, israel, israeli, palestine, palestinian, syria, syrian, turkey, ottoman
Biographies & Memoirs/Historical/Military & Wars/Afghan & Iraq Wars/Afghan War	afghan war
Biographies & Memoirs/Historical/Military & Wars/Afghan & Iraq Wars/Iraq War	iraq war
Biographies & Memoirs/Historical/Military &	civil war

Wars/American Civil War	
Biographies & Memoirs/Historical/Military & Wars/American Revolution	american revolution, american revolution war
Biographies & Memoirs/Historical/Military & Wars/Branches/Air Force	air force
Biographies & Memoirs/Historical/Military & Wars/Branches/Army	army
Biographies & Memoirs/Historical/Military & Wars/Branches/Marines	marine, marines
Biographies & Memoirs/Historical/Military & Wars/Branches/Navy	navy
Biographies & Memoirs/Historical/Military & Wars/Cold War	cold war
Biographies & Memoirs/Historical/Military & Wars/Vietnam War	vietnam war
Biographies & Memoirs/Historical/Military & Wars/World War I	world war 1, world war I, WW1
Biographies & Memoirs/Historical/Military & Wars/World War II	world war 2, world war II, WW2
Biographies & Memoirs/Leaders & Notable People/Presidents & Heads of State/British Prime Ministers	united kingdom prime minister, UK prime minister, U.K. prime minister, british prime minister, great britain prime minister
Biographies & Memoirs/Leaders & Notable People/Presidents & Heads of State/US Presidents	united states president, US president, U.S. president, american president
Biographies & Memoirs/Leaders & Notable People/Religious/Buddhism	buddhist, buddhism
Biographies & Memoirs/Leaders & Notable	catholic, catholicism

People/Religious/Catholicism	
Biographies & Memoirs/Leaders & Notable People/Religious/Christianity	christian, christianity
Biographies & Memoirs/Leaders & Notablo People/Religious/Hinduism	hindu, hinduism
Biographies & Memoirs/Leaders & Notable People/Religious/Islam	islam, islamic, islamist
Biographies & Memoirs/Leaders & Notable People/Religious/Judaism	judaism
Biographies & Memoirs/Sports & Outdoor/Baseball [alias]	baseball
Biographies & Memoirs/Sports & Outdoor/Basketball [alias]	basketball
Biographies & Memoirs/Sports & Outdoor/Boxing [alias]	box, boxing
Biographies & Memoirs/Sports & Outdoor/Football [alias]	football, american football
Biographies & Memoirs/Sports & Outdoor/Golf [alias]	golf
Biographies & Memoirs/Sports & Outdoor/Hockey [alias]	hockey
Biographies & Memoirs/Sports & Outdoor/Motor Sports [alias]	motor sport, f1, formula 1, formula one, nascar, grand prix
Biographies & Memoirs/Sports & Outdoor/Rugby [alias]	rugby
Biographies & Memoirs/Sports & Outdoor/Soccer [alias]	soccer
UK-specific keywords:	
Biography & True Accounts/Arts & Literature/Composers & Musicians/Classical	classic composer, classic music, classical composer, classicial music
Biography & True Accounts/Arts & Literature/Composers & Musicians/Country & Folk/Country	country music, country band, country artist
Biography & True Accounts/Arts & Literature/Composers & Musicians/Country & Folk/Folk	folk music, folk singer, folk artist, folk band

Biography & True Accounts/Arts & Literature/Composers & Musicians/Jazz	jazz band, jazz artist, jazz music
Biography & True Accounts/Arts & Literature/Composers & Musicians/Pop	pop music, pop artist, pop band, pop singer
Biography & True Accounts/Arts & Literature/Composers & Musicians/Rhythm & Blues	r&b, r & b, rhythm & blues
Biography & True Accounts/Arts & Literature/Composers & Musicians/Rock	rock & roll, rock music, rock band, rock genre
Biography & True Accounts/Arts & Literature/Dancers	dancer, dancing, ballet, choreography, choreographer
Biography & True Accounts/Historical/Holocaust	holocaust
Biography & True Accounts/Historical/Military & Wars/American Civil War	american civil war
Biography & True Accounts/Historical/Military & Wars/American Revolution	american revolution war
Biography & True Accounts/Historical/United Kingdom	british, scotland, scottish, north ireland, wales, welsh, united kingdom
Biography & True Accounts/Historical/United States	united states
Biography & True Accounts/Leaders & Notable People/Presidents & Heads of State/US Presidents	US president, U.S. president, america president
Biography & True Accounts/Leaders & Notable People/Royalty/British Royalty	british royalty, british monarchy, british king, british queen, british prince, british princess, british duchess, england royalty, england monarchy, england king, england queen, england prince, england princess, england duchess, english royalty, english monarchy, english king, english queen, english prince, english princess, english, duchess

Biography & True Accounts/Professionals & Academics/Astronauts	astronaut, apollo, nasa
Biography & True Accounts/Regional U.K.	british, scotland, scottish, north ireland, wales, welsh
Biography & True Accounts/Sport & Outdoor/American Football [alias]	united states football, america football, american football
Biography & True Accounts/Sport & Outdoor/Football [alias]	soccer, football
Biography & True Accounts/Sport & Outdoor/Motor Sports [alias]	motor sport, motor sports, f1, formula one, formula 1, nascar, grand prix

Appendix F
49 Free Websites That Will Promote Your Free Book

Now that you've paid the editor, proof reader and cover illustrator, money is pretty tight. so, if there are places where you can promote or advertise you book for free, you should make the most of it. The following table is a comprehensive list of websites that will actively push your book to their followers. They often have well developed email lists with undisclosed numbers of followers that are regularly sent newsletters to targeted genre audiences. The best time to use these sites is when you have a free or discounted period scheduled for your book. These websites will work for you to get it in front of a wider audience. Paid advertising and sites that request 'donations' to guarantee listing are not included in this list. There are many social media groups and communities where you can manually plug your book, but they often get saturated by authors and don't necessarily reach readers.

How to use the following table

- Do not work your way through the list and submit your book everywhere. It won't be relevant to every site and you will waste your time

- Begin by making a primary list of sites that are relevant to your book genre, price and target audience. Each individual site has their own criteria for inclusion - do some homework and check your book fits their criteria

- Explore the sites you are interested in by subscribing to their emails and reading their recent posts. If the site isn't very active on social media then your exposure will not be as far reaching as you hope

- A general guide to the volume of followers for each site is included so that you have a better idea of the potential reach for your promotion. These figures change rapidly as sites are discovered and shared, so the figures listed here will already have changed, but only in a positive way!

- Plan your KDP or discounted periods ahead of schedule. Most sites need a certain amount of notice before they can list your book.

A final few thoughts

- Inclusion is not always guaranteed

-

- Sites listed appear to be genuine and recently active. Many I have tried and tested myself.

- Some sites include perma-free books, others do not. Most prefer a book that is listed free, or at the very least discounted

-

- Codes used for the followers: FB - Facebook, TW - Twitter, P - Pinterest, G+ - Google+

- Blank squares in the table indicate that no information was available

- If you come across any additional sites or corrections, please let me know - designteam@noveldesignstudio.com

    You can download a clickable version of the following table by going
here:

    www.smarturl.it/APMFreepromo

Name	Genre	Book Price	Submission Requirements	Followers
Addicted to eBooks	Any except erotica	Free (regular price must be $5.99 or less)	Must have at least 5 Amazon US reviews	FB 8,500+, TW 2,700+
Authors Den	Any	Any		FB 4700+
Awesome Gang	Any	Any		TW 4,200+ FB 6,400+ G+ 400+
Black Caviar Bookclub	Any	Free		FB 210+ TW 24000+ P 5060+ G+ 750+
Book Angel	Any except explicit	Free		TW 20+
Book Deal Hunter	Any	Free	2 days notice	FB 1300+
Book Goodies	Any	Free	Think 2-3 weeks ahead. No shortcode urls allowed.	FB 5,000+ TW 6,000+ P 300+
Book Goodies for Kids	Childrens Books	Free	Suitable for 18 and under	FB 980+ TW 410+ P 10+
Book Hitch	Any	Any		FB 140+ TW 460+ Blogger 5+
Book Matchers	Any	Any		
Book Pinning	Any except erotica or horror	Any	No reposting within 30 days	FB7600+ TW 540+ P 240+ G+ 20+
Content Mo	Any	Free		3 FB pages 330+ TW 3000+
eBook Lister	Any except erotica	Free or bargain	Up to 60 days in advance. 25 hours to get book listed. Star ratings of 3 or above	FB 200+ Genre specific emails
eBooks Habit	Any except erotica	Free	3 Reviews	FB 1500+
eReader Girl	Non-fiction, children's ebooks and Christian fiction	Free	24 hours notice	FB 6800+ TW 740+
eReader News Today	Any	Free	Send in 3 days	FB 459300+

			before book goes free. Over 3 reviews and 4 star rating	
	except erotica			
eReader Utopia	Any except erotica	Free	One post every 3 months Will not accept books with 3 star average	FB 15900+ Site 100+ TW 2100+
eReading on the Cheap	Any	Free or cheap	Need at least 3 days notice Cannot submit same book more than once every 3 months	10,000+ Added to Daily Deals newsletter, Twitter & FB
Erotica Every Day	Erotica	Free or bargain		FB 3400+
Free & Discounted Books	Any	Any		FB 2700+ TW 5,200+ G+ 7,800+ P 3,900+
Freebies 4 Mom	Any	Free		P 18100+ TW 118600+ G+ 2800+
Free Book Club	Any except Erotica	Free		FB 12300+ TW 3060+
Free Books	Any	Free		FB 650+
Free Booksy	Any except Erotica	Free		FB 88500+ TW 6900+
Free Stuff Times	Any	Free		FB 44200+ TW 98300+ Site 3000+ P 220+ G+ 300+
Frugal Tips & Freebies	Any	Free		FB 28800+ TW 4900+ G+ 1000+ P 875+
Great Books Great Deals (Link for Author Promotions Form)	Any except non fiction, children's books, erotica, graphic horror	$3.99 or less	Must have 20 reviews and average 4+ stars	3 different Pinterest profiles each with 200+ followers G+ 220+ FB 280+
Hunt 4 Freebies	Any	Free		FB 95100+ TW 9800+

				P 2400+ G+ 4900+
iAuthor	Any except Erotica	Any	High resolution images	
iLove eBooks	Any	Free		FB 18700+ TW 30+ P 980+
Indie Book of the Day	Any except erotica	Free	At least 2 days notice. 3.5 review rating or above	FB 1700+ TW 1100+
Indie Heart	Any except Erotica, Christian Fiction, Childrens Book and Non fiction	Free		FB 20+
Jogena	Any	Any		
Jungle Deals and Steals	Any except Paranorm al or horror	Free		FB 2700+
Just Kindle Books	Any	Free or discounted		FB 6800+
Kobo Book Hub	Any	Any	Kobo format	FB 80+ TW 1900+
Korner Konnection	Any	Any	Indie Authors	FB 10,500+
Launch Effect	Mystery, Suspense, Thriller	$2.99 or less, incl free	10 reviews one book per author per month	FB 200+ TW 80+
Nerd Girl	Any	Any		FB - 5400+ TW - 1600+
One Hundred Free Books	Any	Free or Perma Free		FB 88300+ Email list 17600+ TW 3700+ G+ 3200+ P 2800+
Pretty Hot	Romance and Erotica	Any		
Read Cheaply	Any	Free or discounted	Good Reviews. Books $2.99 or less Post about the site on your website and social media, then paste the	FB 130+ TW 50+

			url when you submit your book.	
Snickslist	Any except Erotica	Free - KDP Select days	Only for 1-5 days in line with the KDP select days.	
The eReader Cafe	Any except Erotica and short stories	Free or bargains	Submit at least 3 days before promotions	FB 60100+ TW 1800+ P 820+
The Virtual Bookcase	Any	Any		Followers 2500+
Wanton Reads	Romance, erotica,	Any		TW 140+ FB 860+
What to Read after Fifty Shades	Erotica	Any		FB 85800+
Wise Grey Owl	Any	Any		FB 270 TW 2600+
Zwoodle Books	Any except erotica	Free	Average 4+ stars	P 30+ FB 30+ TW 960+

Appendix G
Download Addresses

Amazon Associates
https://affiliate-program.amazon.com/

Amazon Cart
http://www.amazon.com/gp/socialmedia/amazoncart/ref=amazoncart_surl_a
mazoncartlp

Author Central Page
https://authorcentral.amazon.com

Amazon Tools and Resources
To download Kindle Previewer, Kindle Kids' Book Creator, Kindle Textbook
Creator, Kindle Comic Creator
https://kdp.amazon.com/help?topicId=A3IWA2TQYMZ5J6

ISBN Numbers
www.isbn.org

KDP Account
https://kdp.amazon.com/

Kindle Scout
https://kindlescout.amazon.com/submit

Kindle World
https://kindleworlds.amazon.com/

The following downloadable pdf files will help in preparing your book:

Fiction Categories
www.smarturl.it/APMFictionCat

Juvenile Fiction Categories
www.smarturl.it/APMJuvFicCat

Non-Fiction Categories
www.smarturl.it/APMNonFicCat

Fiction Sub Category Keywords
www.smarturl.it/APMFictionSubCat

Non-Fiction Sub Category Keywords
www.smarturl.it/APMNonFicSubCat

HTML Tag Sheet
www.smarturl.it/APMHTMLTable

49 Free Websites That Will Promote Your Free Book
www.smartulr.it/APMFreepromo